Home Flown

The Laymamma's Guide
to an
Empty Nest

Home Flown

The Laymamma's Guide to an Empty Nest

Glenys Newton

Cover Illustration
Federica Patrone

Talking

Whoever holds the talking
stick has within their
hands the sacred
power of words –   but
only the one   must
who holds the   speak the
stick may   truth about
speak   personal
understanding
and experience

Stick

First published 2014 in Great Britain by
Talking Stick
an imprint of Archive Publishing
Dorset England

For all our titles please go to:
transpersonalbooks.com

A CIP Record for this book is available from
the British Cataloguing in Publication data office

ISBN 978-1-906289-26-3   (Paperback)

To contact the author, please visit her website
www.glenysnewton.co.uk

Printed and bound in Malta
by Melita Press

THE AUTHOR

Glenys worked with horses until becoming a mother in 1989. She thoroughly enjoyed the role of 'Mum' which led to a profound knowledge of football stickers and Ninja Turtles. She then qualified as a social worker, working in mental health and, latterly, in adoption.

When her son left home she decided to pursue her lifelong love of writing and stories. She took a leap of faith and packed in her job; sold the house and did a story-telling course. After a year of living in an old post office van with her eternally patient lurcher dog, Tom, she settled in a beautiful little cottage in North Hertfordshire.

She continues to tell stories, enjoying in particular biographical stories, which has led to the writing of this book. She wished to share her story of her son leaving home and the complicated journey of the nest becoming empty.

The sharing of stories is a great tradition of our land that has been lost in recent years. Thankfully story-telling is making a comeback as people hunger for the treasures that are to be found in the listening and telling of stories. Writing is simply another way of being able to share our stories with other people.

To contact the author, please visit her website:

www.glenysnewton.co.uk or email glenys.newt@gmail.com

DEDICATION

For Chris,
my inspiration and sonshine,
with all my love.

CONTENTS

INTRODUCTION

My son was born 25 years ago. When he was born my life changed irreversibly and there was nothing that anybody could have said or done that could have prepared me for that enormous change. I remember somebody saying to me, when he was born, that I would only ever sleep with one eye shut again and I also remember thinking that they were talking nonsense. It was true.

On becoming a parent there is an internal alarm always ready to go off, no matter how old your child is but especially when you are learning the ropes of how to deal with this little babe in arms.

Much is made of this time and a great deal of attention is drawn to the newborn and the new parents. People feel, understandably, very comfortable in being able to make a grand old fuss. And so they should, as welcoming new life into the world is a time of celebration. What people don't warn you about is how fast that little baby grows up and turns into a big person that leaves home.

Everybody talks of the enormous changes that a newborn brings in to the home but nobody talks of the changes at the other end, when they leave. I found that my son leaving home was a far bigger change than when he was born. I also found that people were far less willing to talk about his departure than his joyful arrival.

What do the words Empty Nest conjure up? Until it happened to me I had never really considered it or the people who were experiencing it. I just thought that it was a natural progression of life, which it is, but never how complicated it is. Despite the fact that we have many years to think about our children leaving home, as with their arrival, there is nothing that can prepare us for it. That was how it felt for me anyway. I was shocked by the enormity of it and by my feelings of grief. There was a multitude of different emotions at play and I didn't really know what to do with them. My boy had flown the nest and I was officially an 'empty nester'.

The dictionary definition of 'empty nest' is 'a household in which one or more parents live after the children have left home'. As a result there is the empty nest syndrome which is not a clinical condition but is a recognised state of being. It is described as 'a feeling of grief and loneliness parents or guardians may feel when their children leave home for the first time'.

Given that 'empty nest' has been awarded a title I was surprised by how little it is talked about. When I looked about for any books on the subject I found a few, but surprisingly few, given that it is something that happens to so many people and how complicated it is. I tried talking to people but there were not many of my friends in a similar situation and they found it impossible to be able to understand. I was the same until I found myself in that situation.

So I have put pen to paper to write down all of the things that I wished that I had known, in the hope that it will be of help to someone else out there. Not all of this may be relevant to everyone, so each person must take what they find interesting or helpful and adapt the rest to their own situation.

Parenting is a complicated job. There are precious few instructions and we tend to base our parenting on our own experiences as children, whether it is to replicate that or to steer as far away as possible from how we were parented. Generally a mixture of the two.

We learn from our friends, neighbours and the media but most of us are making it up as we go along. It involves a lot of thinking on your feet and a huge amount of tolerance, mainly on the part of the child. I do think that, of all the jobs in the world, parenting is probably the only one that you are guaranteed to get wrong in some way, shape or form. It is also one of the few jobs that, if done properly, means that the point will come when you are not needed anymore.

In Western culture, independence from the family home is esteemed and applauded. It is something to be aimed for, whether rightly or wrongly. We raise our children with this in mind somewhere in the background, but this is often taken over by the hurly burly of daily life while they are growing up. Personally, I was so ensconced in the job of being a mum that I could not envisage a day when that might end. While my son was growing up, each day brought on fresh challenges, joys and frustrations which seemed to pack our lives, leaving no gaps for thoughts of twenty years down the line. And then before you know it, your child is leaving home! They are seemingly all grown up.

The ideal of parenting is to guide our children towards an adulthood that will create the most opportunities for them and enable them to be of benefit to this world. At least, that is what we hope for. By guiding them towards adulthood we are naturally preparing them to fly the nest. Each day is an extra lesson in flight. Why, then, is it so shocking when it actually happens? And why does nobody want to talk about it?

I felt that the empty nest experience was one characterised by loss. There were many elements to it but that was the overriding feeling. As with loss of any kind it takes a brave person to be able to listen to somebody else's story and it can seem that within the western culture there is a reluctance to want to burden anyone else with our sad thoughts. We just tend to 'get on with it'. The term 'a stiff upper lip' does not come out of nowhere and that is generally what is expected, in Britain anyway, in the face of any kind of loss or hardship. This can make it hard to find anyone to talk to apart from trusted friends and family.

I had never anticipated the tsunami of different feelings that would blast through me and my life when my nest emptied and I was grappling around for any clues as to what to do. As a parent, a great deal of the day-to-day planning is based around having your child in your home and that places a varying degree of demands upon your time and resources.

Without your child, all this activity is now replaced by a void that needs to be first respected and then filled in some way. I had no idea that this was normal and wondered, at some point, whether I was losing the plot. Many of the people who seemed willing to talk at length about their empty nest experience were the ones who were desperately hanging on to the role of parent and that did not feel particularly healthy either.

I tried to recall my own experience of leaving home but the circumstances were very different and it was difficult to draw comparisons. My experience of being an empty nestee was hurried and premature and I was in a bit of a hurry to see the world. As such I have been interested to ask young people about their experiences of leaving home and they have been enlightening and helpful. I have included a few of their thoughts, which I have found inspiring and which, hopefully, will also be of interest to others. Leaving home is an immensely personal experience but there are often words from others that can resonate with our own experiences.

Leaving home signifies the end of childhood and all the magic that lies within it. Childhood is often spoken of as if it were something generic when it is anything but. Childhood is as individual as each child that lives it. Childhood is the time and place where so many seeds and ideas are planted and nurtured, either lovingly or bitterly, by parents. When our children leave home it is the time for them to take the fully grown plants of those seeds out into the world and make of them what they will and can. It is an exciting time but can also be daunting.

As we parents are being left with a world that is changed, so our children are launching into the great unknown. Suddenly they are being asked, or asking of themselves, to be responsible for themselves and those around them. They are being asked to stop seeing themselves as children. When do we actually stop seeing ourselves as children though? Similarly, there comes a point when we must stop seeing our children as children and see them as the adults that they have become or are becoming. But do we ever stop seeing our children as children?

The years following my son's first launch from the family nest have been varied and colourful. Things are very different now, both for me and for him, and it has been interesting to live the changes that have come about. It has been fun, although I realise that I have been lucky that he has been safe and well. The fear of our children coming to any harm remains whatever age they are. My responsibility towards his well-being has, though, lessened as the years have gone by and he has marched his way to adulthood.

I have noticed that there are many phases to the whole empty nest experience. Each phase brings about its own set of complications and merits and it is with the benefit of hindsight that I am able to see the logic of their sequence. The passing of time is such a wonderful thing! As such, I have divided the chapters into the different phases, as I saw them, with valuable input from other parents and young people. I have tried to ask the views of dads as well although, purely unintentionally, this is a book that has ended up being largely aimed at mums. I am a mum and it seems that the people on empty nest discussion forums on the internet are, in the majority, mums. It may be because, very generally, they tend to be the ones who spend more time with the children while they are growing up so feel their loss differently when they leave. I am happy for this to be contradicted but I am just going on what I have found out there while talking to people about the whole empty nest experience.

So, for all those empty nesters out there, this is for you! All ye magnificent people who now enter a different phase of life. Who are being asked to wriggle out of a well-fitting and familiar skin and into the unknown, and not breathe a murmur about it. Who are expected to carry on as though life has not been up-ended. It is not all doom and gloom and, indeed, there is a great deal of humour to be had as children grow and leave the family home. A whole raft of new experiences to be had. But before they leave they need to prepare to leave, and the run up to departure is a whole phase in its own right.

CHAPTER 1

THE RUN UP TO DEPARTURE

The run up to departure is a time for our children to start flapping their wings and preparing for flight. In reality they are doing that from day one. From the very beginning of their lives we are doing that in preparing our children for independence. It starts with children learning to feed themselves, tie their own shoelaces and learning to do things for themselves. It then progresses towards them having a bath on their own, then going to school on their own and learning to spend time on their own. As parents we celebrate each milestone as it happens. It is celebrated because that is the point of parenting, to enable our children to manage on their own.

We actively encourage our children to be able to carry out tasks independently and pride ourselves as parents when they are able to do so. All that bragging at the school gates about whose child does what. All those beaming smiles at toddler groups when your child is the first to do something. Announcements of 'My Clarissa can play Mozart's 5th on 17 different instruments'. That's what it's all about. Well mostly. Some people actually just like showing off.

All of these milestones are leading up to our children becoming independent and eventually leaving home. In fact, one of the extremely helpful things to be getting on with in the run up to departure is to teach our children domestic chores. How to pay bills, cook, hoover, clean the loo, anticipate running out of milk and all of those daily tasks that we take for granted and seem so obvious. They are only obvious because we do them every day. It is well worth pointing out how they are done, and delegating some of the jobs to our children so that they become second nature rather than something else that has to be learnt at a time when so many other things are new in their lives — when they eventually live independently.

How to boil up a pot of pasta may seem simple but it needs to be taught and learnt. How to not run out of loo roll might appear obvious but it takes time to learn that there is not actually a loo roll fairy conjuring up fresh supplies. How to make cheap food that will not leave them with multi vitamin deficiencies is helpful. Whether the advice is heeded is another matter. Being gifted the capacity to be self-sufficient is something that they can take with them and is an extra tool in the tool kit to carry out of the door as they go.

As I have said, parenting is one of the few jobs where, if done properly and the circumstances allow, we are not needed any more. Although each milestone achieved is greeted with a cheerful hurray, there is also a little bit of us inside that twinges with the realisation that each new skill is a step further away from us being needed any more. That and a sense of shared pride. Despite feeling proud every time that our children are able to manage without us there is also a sense of increasing loss. Nostalgia, and the relief of being freed from duties, seem to be the hallmarks of parenting.

I think that all parents can find themselves looking back at their child's early years with fond memories while also remembering how tiring it could be at times. We may have all, at some point during the younger years, sat down at the end of an exhausting day and vowed to be super-duper parents the next day and not get irritable even once and promised ourselves to relish the magic that is our children.

Pre-children, people often fantasise about spending days doing play-doh activities, happily pushing their child on a swing, reading under a softly-lit lamp while the child snuggles into you. Pre-children, people often stare accusingly at parents who threaten their children with limb removal if they ask one more time for an ice cream. It is incredibly easy to bring up other people's children. We are also fed romantic images of parenthood that we aspire to until the reality hits. It all sounds so easy until you are in the middle of it and caught up in the busyness of each day.

Despite all the exhaustion and tedium, being a parent is one of the most amazing experiences that a person can have in any one lifetime. There does not seem to be anything to compare it to, as corny as that might sound. For me, as much as there were times when it felt that all of the plates could have come crashing to the ground at any moment, there was not a single day that I regretted being a parent. I loved it. I also sit with the benefit of hindsight and of perhaps having my rose-tinted glasses firmly in place! Whilst I loved being a mum, I can also remember times when it felt tedious and relentless. I can conjure up easily the memory of sinking into the sofa at the end of another day, absolutely shattered. The relief I felt when my son had gone to bed and I could get a bit of time to myself, little realising that time goes by quickly and that soon I would have more of that time to myself than I would ever have hoped for.

I do remember being in a supermarket one day negotiating the aisles with gritted teeth and a stroppy toddler when a lady wistfully told me how quickly a child's years go by. At the time I felt that it was going anything but quickly. I was baffled by how she could ever think that going round the supermarket, juggling all the things that need juggling during a child's early years and also finding the time to sew name tags into another new P.E. kit could be something that was going past quickly. I have now become that middle-aged lady peering at children in buggies and telling the parents to enjoy the young years while they can as they go so quickly. Wagging my finger and issuing time warnings in a knowing and possibly slightly creepy manner. But blink indeed and you miss it. The years whizz on by and before you know it your dear sweet little child person has turned into a great big person with a life that is becoming increasingly independent from your own.

Once upon a time you could have accounted for each second of your child's day. It was there in the school newsletters, going to different activities, finding things to do in the holidays that didn't cost a kidney and generally being very present. The time passes and then more and more you have to ask them what they have been doing each day. As they grow older you are no longer a part of their activities. You may still be a taxi resource but they begin to organise their own lives into which you are now slotted rather than being the focus of. There have to be catch-up sessions so that everyone knows what everyone else is doing throughout the day and how things might also be changing for your child.

During the years leading up to adolescence your child begins to focus on their peers and you start to take a back seat. Well, you take a back seat in everything except for driving them to places, providing pizzas, funding and general usefulness — rather than being someone with whom everything is done and/or coordinated. Your child starts to juggle his identity with those of his/her friends and it is time for you, as a parent, to back off a little bit. You still need to be there but usually at a time when it suits them. This is not them being selfish; it is just the way things are and the way that things should be. Sometimes it can feel as though you hardly know this person that was once encased in a dear sweet little toddler body but is now roaming around the home in a gangly body that does not seem to altogether fit together properly. As much as it can feel as though we have lost touch with our little child that once was, it can also feel like that for them too.

There is no doubt that the teenage years can be turbulent ones. If we try, we can all remember that feeling of not fitting into your own skin and of being completely misunderstood. That time of life when there is a force shield separating you from the rest of the world. It can feel as though there is a whole life ahead but you are not quite sure how to get to it. That there is an amazing life to be had and someone else is living it or that you are being stopped from living it in some way. For young people, at some point, it can feel that their parents are the only thing standing between them and their future. Parents can be a block to be removed, a hurdle to be overcome.

We know, having lived those years, that it is possible to survive but they do not know that yet so we need to help them through it. Or they may know it — but it is difficult to remember when you are in the middle of what feels like an emotional whirlpool. The problems of the moment are all-encompassing in those years and it feels impossible that ordinary life could be continuing in the light of all that angst. Whatever is happening at the time, be it issues with a girlfriend or boyfriend or troubles with friends, can completely and utterly, albeit temporarily, take over all life and thoughts. I can remember incidents in my teenage years that seem relatively minor looking back but that, at the time, felt insurmountable, the end of the world and that nobody could possibly know how difficult it was. And I guess they didn't. Can it ever really be possible to know how another person is living their thoughts?

When your child is going through those years you end up living their torment by proxy in one way or another. There is a saying 'You are only ever as happy as your saddest child' and that just about sums it up really. It is very difficult to be living a happy and carefree life when you know that your child is unhappy or uncomfortable with themselves and the world around them. It is not a given that every teenager has to be miserable and pacing around with a black heart but they can be bumpy years. They are years of grappling with an identity, of putting together all that has been learnt so far and trying to make sense of it all. Years of feeling misunderstood and trying to find a direction in life.

Adolescence is actually a relatively recent concept. As recently as 100 years ago the term adolescence was not in common usage. Maybe it was because children went out to work at an earlier age and skipped the interim years, going straight from child to adult. Maybe life was seemingly more straightforward. Ongoing research into the workings of the brain at various stages of life has helped us to recognise that the brain during the adolescent years is still taking shape. It has helped us to know that there is no such thing as a simple leap from childhood to adulthood. As life has generally improved for our children, as a whole, I can only speculate that the recognition of the adolescent years is a good thing.

The run up to leaving home is an accumulation of the teenage years. It is the launch pad. It is the runway paved with everything that will prepare them for their initial flight from the nest. It can feel like a long and drawn out launch pad and, for parents, feel peppered with a sensation of being punished for something though you are not quite sure what it is.

Although the years may feel as though they are dragging on, they do end up speeding past quickly. Retrospectively they are important years that carve the way to future relationships with your children. At times it can feel impossible to have a relationship with this difficult being that is galumphing about the house and not being particularly cooperative. It can feel as though the sooner they are out of your sight then the better it is for everyone but these moments are generally only fleeting. Intense but fleeting. Surfing the waves of these years takes patience and resilience on the parts of everyone involved and I am sure we can all look back at our teenage years and think of a few toe-curling incidents that we would rather had not happened.

The relationship with your adolescent child can feel as though it is made up of one long round of nagging and clashing of ideals. Our ideal may be that we would not want the household supply of mugs to be ensconced beneath piles of laundry in their bedroom while their ideal is a million miles from this, focusing on socialising either via technology or in person. A request to do some menial household task may cause a reaction equal to that of being requested to plough the entire region with their bare hands. You start to lose perspective of what constitutes a reasonable request. Surely a reasonable request would not elicit such an extreme response? It can feel impossible to comprehend how this dear person that you have raised with such love and tenderness is able to approach a simple request with such lack of reasoning.

Even the very nicest of people in the world are in some sort of bubble at that age, encased by some impenetrable layer that can prevent any level of decent compromise and communication. The more you try the more baffled they become. The more you insist, then the more you are distanced from the cute person that you thought you knew so well and with whom you have shared the same living space for all these years. How can this be? Sometimes the dear sweet person of yesteryear pokes their head out through the hormonal cloud and a little burst of music heralds forth from inside your maternal heart. There they are! A parent's heart has a satnav that is never wrong! Or is it? How can it have come to this? Surely we were not that bad to our parents? We probably were and, in many cases, a lot worse.

It is helpful to have a benchmark as a point of moral departure to rein ourselves in from incessant grumbling. It is also helpful to find someone who is having a worse time than you. Everything is relative and this puts things into perspective fairly quickly. Get together with parents of other teenagers and you will soon find that yours is far more reasonable than you have been imagining. A chat with other parents and you will soon be able to dig out a few positives. I am painting a gloomy picture! Although it is not all doom and gloom throughout the adolescent years, it can certainly be a rocky time for all concerned and at times it can feel as though there are long gaps between laughter. How bumpy and how smooth is as varied as mankind itself. My dad used to call it the 14 to 18 war but it is quite possible, rare but possible, that you live in perfect harmony throughout.

In the same way that childhood is often viewed as something that is generic, adolescents can be also viewed as a homogenous group, which they certainly are not. No one person is the same as anyone else at any point in their lives. The spectrum of behaviour among adolescents is as wide and long as the universe itself, but it is during these years that our children are trying to begin to inch away from us aboard a truck full of hormones. The years leading up to departure, and ultimately independence, are mighty different from the toddler years although at times it can feel as though you are dealing with a toddler.

During the younger years there is a general day-to-day encouraging to eat broccoli, do homework, have a wash, practise the trumpet and whatever else may be going on in your lives. All of those years seem to have a clear focus and one of the main aims is to keep your child safe at a time when they are unable to do so themselves. Although tremendously time-consuming and varied there is an element of those parenting years which is mildly predictable in what is expected of everyone all round.

It is a relationship of total dependence on the child's part towards the parent, which then needs to morph into something else. It is actually incredible to think of the changes that take place within the relationship between parent and child and that those changes take place within a relatively few years. A parent needs to move from changing a child's nappy, mashing up their food and encouraging them to eat vegetables to a relationship that moves towards independence. It is, perhaps, the only relationship in our lives that needs to change to such an extent from its beginnings.

The run up to departure years are when the gears shift towards independence and you may find yourself going at a different pace to your child. The point is that you are moving from a position of total authority towards one of equality and that takes a few trial runs and hiccups. The matters of eating healthily, having a wash, clearing up and all of the daily needs that propel us towards a functioning adulthood are still important but it is not as easy to persuade them to do these things. It is equally difficult to sit back and watch them not being done.

Although it is, of course, up to every teenager to organise their own lives to some degree, it can be nigh on impossible not to intervene when it is quite clear that they are letting everything pile up around their ears. They tell us not to nag and moan but that can feel practically impossible. The bottom line is we do it because we care; otherwise it would be an awful lot easier not to say anything at all. A large part of this is not about what is being done or achieved or not being done and not achieved, but the attitude with which this is being done or not done. The aim as parents is to install an attitude in our children that will stand them in good stead in the future although it may not always feel like it at the time. The rewards, as many of the rewards in parenting, are in the long term. It is probably the biggest investment that we will make in our lifetimes.

During the run up to departure you are given the almighty task of continually reminding your child of all those precious values that you have taken such pains to install and that are seemingly pointless and irrelevant at a time of your child's life when they are least interested in what you have to say. It can feel that the child that we have always known and loved has been kidnapped and replaced by an alien but fear not, it is temporary! As hard as it can seem at the time it is worth hanging on to the thought that it is not forever. These years can also set the pace for later years. How we react to them, and manage the challenges that they present, can resonate for years afterwards. I know that it took many years for me to feel comfortable with my family following the teenage years and it was credit to everyone concerned that we all got past it eventually.

I do believe that relationships between young people and their parents have shifted slightly now and there is a move towards a level of communication between the generations that was not there, on the whole, with previous generations. There does not seem to be such a gulf between parents and children, although this may be what every generation of parent thinks. It does feel that parents are generally more involved with their children while growing up rather than playing a largely supervisory role.

Parents have spoken to me of how, when they were growing up, they would generally spend their leisure time with peers and siblings rather than their parents, to whom they would return for mealtimes or if they needed something. As parents themselves, they have spoken of how they spend time with their children playing games or going out doing activities, which was not something that their parents would do with them. Maybe it is because parents have more time to spend with their children now or maybe it is because there is a different attitude to parenting than in previous generations.

When I was a teenager, being seen out with your parents would have rung the social death knell but now it is common for teenagers and their parents to go out together. Whatever changes may have come about — and I believe that they are, on the whole, positive — it is still important to acknowledge the difference between the generations rather than try to 'keep up'. However much we may be closer with our children than we were with our parents, we are still their parents. It is a time in a child's life when they are trying to separate themselves from their parents to carve out their own identity.

At this point, a young person is still seeking guidance (however grudgingly) rather than a mate to go clubbing with. It is also a time when parents start to become a bit of an embarrassment so it is probably not the ideal time to suggest a night out with their friends. Being an embarrassment to your children can have its own entertainment value though. My dad used to take me to school on an old 1928 Sunbeam motorbike and sidecar. I was mortified and would want to be dropped off down the road. Despite striving to be an individual, most teenagers just do not want to stand out in any way and do whatever they can just to 'fit in'. The teenage years are a sea of opposites and oxymorons that refuse to roll over and behave. My dad would insist on dropping me off right in front of the school, in front of everyone and to much applause. In hindsight I can see how much he enjoyed this. In hindsight I can also see that he wanted to share with me his passion of motorbikes, which then fuelled a lifetime love of the open road for me, and a hankering for travel.

So, rather than encroaching upon their world, it is a good time to find that something that you may have always had in common and keep doing it. In fact, this is now an ideal opportunity to enjoy with your teenage offspring anything that you may have had in common with your child. It is something that links you to the past, and times shared and spent together and will also link into the future, forming a bridge between the worlds that you are temporarily living. It is great to be able to spend time with your dear person, who is frantically flapping their wings, and be able to hear how they may be trying to make sense of the world. A time when thoughts and ideas can be exchanged naturally rather than having to have official sit downs for discussions.

It is fascinating to hear their ideas and be inspired by their enthusiasm for something that you may not have thought of before. A teenager, despite all talk to the contrary, is a fount of wisdom. It is at this time of life that they believe any ideas they have are unique to them — they are the first person in the world ever to have had that idea. If only we could harness and bottle that enthusiasm and sense of wonder. There is a pure sense of injustice that becomes jaded in later years through experience and a feeling of helplessness of how you, as one person, can bring about any change in the world. In teenage worlds there are no such barriers and I believe that there is much that we, as adults, could learn from that.

Despite all the bravado shown by our teenage offspring, it is without doubt a time of fears and question marks. My son has spoken of it feeling like a time full of apprehension and excitement at the same time. He was thoroughly fed up with school and so, once he had left, was excited at not having to do that anymore while also being nervous about taking a running jump into the unknown. It is a time of life when children are leaving the structure and nurturing of their home and surroundings and are ready to leave all that behind. At few times in our lives do we have to face such a crossroads.

Another young person, who was leaving home to start university, has spoken of being excited about leaving home as she was going to do something new and adventurous and that it was something that she wanted to do. She also knew that she would miss home and the people that made up her home, which felt like the price she had to pay for leaving. She did not feel any great sense of relief at leaving home; rather she was worried that she would get homesick or that she would not meet new people that she could get on with.

The run up to departure can be, and naturally is, very different for each family. For some it is a planned event and the child is supported and nurtured through each step of the journey. For others it can be a fractious time that can lead to a departure that is less than ideal for all concerned. I can safely say that mine was one of those and it has taken time and effort for me not to taint my son's teenage years with my own. One of the things that I have found helpful is the use of rituals. I do not mean the sacrificing of sheep at the bottom of the garden but something simple that marks the passing of time.

Rituals mark the passing of one phase of life to the next and acknowledge the changing nature of the parent-child relationship. It can be a marker in time to allow people to move on to the next step. It can simply be going away for a weekend somewhere or even just a couple of hours put to one side to do something special. Or inviting friends round to have a gathering to mark the occasion. It does not have to be anything elaborate but just something that specifically acknowledges the changing nature of the relationship and the fact that your child is no longer a child as such. Rituals like these can take away the need for much stroppy behaviour and exchanging of unpleasantries. A lot of exasperating and annoying behaviour that we find so difficult to deal with is simply a young person trying to say something that they feel unable to say; or maybe they do not even know what it is they want to say. I am sure that any parent can think up moments when they have been baffled by their child's behaviour and reactions. It might be that they simply want it acknowledged that they are no longer a child. How many times is the protest of 'I'm not a baby you know!' responded to with 'Well stop behaving like one then!'

Easing themselves from the clutches of the home and family is not an easy task and rituals help nudge somebody over the threshold into the next phase of life. Traditionally it might be going to the pub on their 18th to be able to buy their first drink, at least their first legal drink, or keys to the door at 21. A lot of folk are long gone by the age of 21 now so what was once traditional may need adapting to the changing times. When my son was in his early teens I was lucky enough to be able to take him away for a couple of months on an amazing journey. I wanted to spend time with him that wasn't just about doing homework and clearing clothes up off of the floor. I wanted to get to know him again, to hear what he was making of the world without the mundanities of every day getting in the way. This was premature for the run up to departure phase but it certainly gave us something to fall back on when things weren't quite so harmonious on the home front in later years.

In other cultures it is probably better organised and as a person becomes a teenager or starts to have thoughts that their parents are not of this world, they go off and live with their uncle and go and kill a wart-hog or something. There is a line to aim for and to be able to cross to step into some sort of adulthood. Within the western culture, rites of passage are more vague although there are events, such as birthdays and getting a driving licence, that are commonly celebrated. It can feel, though, that we are meandering our way towards adulthood without any great sense of having arrived anywhere. As parents we tend to limp our way to some sort of ill-defined finishing post and there is nothing to say that parents and children will be marching to the same drumbeat along the way.

There may be times during the run up to departure when the memories of that gorgeous toddler that so melted your heart will be a million miles from your mind and this is how it should be. Everyone becoming grumpy with one another is a perfectly natural and helpful part of the whole process. The harder someone is to live with then the easier it is to let them go and that goes for both parents and children.

One mum told me that she felt it was the right time for her daughter to leave and that she felt that her daughter was ready to step out into the world on her own. In fact, both mother and daughter said that, at the time, they were glad to see the back of one another. By the time your teenager has sat for some months, or even years, in their bedroom preening their feathers to fly the nest to the sound of something with a heavy bass line to it, then you are probably ready for them to go too. Not only are you ready, but there are moments when you would positively embrace it! Another mum told me that she cannot wait to have the house to herself and that she feels that she has done her years of parenting and just wants to get on with her life.

Although we tend to focus on the losses it is worth taking a moment to look at the gains that could lie ahead. All of those little niggling things that lead to domestic discord will be no longer. You can look forward to listening to whatever radio station you want. You can sit in silence without the tub thump of some indiscernible noise making its way through the kitchen ceiling. You can be guaranteed that any cereal boxes in the cupboard will not be empty. There are only those brief years during the teenage spell that a person will think that it is acceptable to put an empty cereal box back in the cupboard or an empty milk bottle back in the fridge. Why do they do that?! When all of these little things keep happening we can begin to wish and yearn for an irritation-free existence as the previous mum expressed so wistfully.

But all of these things that we yearn for would also mean being without our children. It is a prospect that we face with a melee of different emotions that swirl about on a daily basis. The accumulation of irritating incidents is designed to make the whole process easier. There is a future that needs to happen. We all need to go our separate ways and we just need enough empty cereal packets and empty milk bottles in order to be able to want that to happen. If we all continued to get along just fine then it might be that nobody would ever go anywhere. Part of the attractiveness of moving towards independence is to escape from the feeling of being confined by your current situation and believing that bigger and better things are waiting out there in the big parent-free world. This is a major incentive to leaving home. So not only are we starting to get slightly irritated by them but they start to get irritated by us.

Ahead lie so many possibilities, and the truth of the matter is that parents and their children need to separate for those possibilities to spring to life. I do think that in past generations it was a lot easier for children to separate themselves from their parents. It used to be enough for a young person to dress differently from their parent and that would automatically differentiate and separate them. Now that different generations can dress the same and that all ages generally have access to the same resources, it does feel as though young people have to think up more and more complicated ways of separating themselves from their parents.

There will always be a way and there will always be music that manages to successfully divide up the generations and it is up to the parents to respect that and to not encroach upon territory that a young person is trying to carve out for themselves, unless they are specifically invited. While it is a great thing to be able to share a love of music, clothes, sport or whatever it may be between parent and child, a young person has to have an area of their life that is unknown to their parents otherwise they never have the room to explore who they are in their own right. During this important time of self-discovery it is not helpful if we are an overwhelming presence that invades every aspect of their lives. A young person may then have to think up ever more complicated measures to gain their own bit of personal space.

And so the run up to departure commences with a sprinkling of huffing and puffing on everyone's parts. It is beautifully designed to ease us gently into separation. We start off by thinking that it is something that would be intensely difficult. As one mum told me 'I dread her leaving. It sits like a lead weight at the bottom of my stomach'. A smattering of door slamming and we begin to think that maybe it is not such a bad plan after all. A few doses of one syllable responses and we begin positively to embrace the thought that our children will be venturing off one day. Any grumpy moments are designed to help us all let go of one another and start the next phase of our lives.

There is also all of the preparation for departure, which can be a very exciting time. As parents we are being introduced to a whole new world of universities, jobs, travelling and experiences that we may not have come across before. There is the weighing of rucksacks, packing of bags and gathering of items that will be useful and 'you will definitely need that' to go through with them and it is fun. Preparing for a whole new life, whatever it may be, is exciting and it is hard not to get caught up in the whirliness of it all.

There then comes the time for everyone to say their goodbyes and ideally this can be done while leaving the metaphorical and physical door open for them to return whenever they would like or need to. Parenting, as we know it up until this point, has reached its natural conclusion and the child that was has grown a full set of wings and is ready to fly.

CHAPTER 2

THE IMMEDIATE AFTERMATH

The immediate aftermath of a child having left home is complicated. There is, of course, some sadness but it is not as simple as that. The absolute immediate aftermath is generally lived through a wall of tears. There is that moment of saying goodbye to your child and, no matter what the circumstances, it can feel as though a limb has been torn off.

One mum said that she would never have believed that it could be so difficult and that it physically hurt when she left her daughter in her new university accommodation. I can remember a feeling of dread and panic as my son walked through the departure gates at the airport when he was leaving for his first trip away from home. I felt actual physical pain and aching. It felt as though the cord between me and my son was stretching beyond its capacity and that at any moment I was going to get pinged up into the sky and stuck to the plane that was transporting him to the other side of the planet. It seemed perfectly possible that I would be found glued to the window of the plane with eyes wildly staring at my offspring.

Almost every parent that I have spoken to has recounted incidents of that heart-wrenching moment of separation and the tears that followed. Even the most sceptical among them were reduced to a blubbering mass while they pulled over in a lay-by somewhere, unable to see through the tears to drive.

One mum said that she felt fine at the actual time of separation but that she stopped to buy something to eat on the way home and broke down in tears in the shop and abandoned her shopping basket in the aisle. She was surprised by her reaction as it had not been a harmonious few years leading up to her son's departure and she had thought that she would just feel relief that it was over.

Each parent that I spoke to had a story to tell, each as individual as the people that they are. The one common factor was that the moment of separation was far harder than they had imagined.

One of my reactions, when my son left home, was 'Who am I going to hide behind now?' This took me totally by surprise, as I hadn't even realised that that was what I had been doing in the first place. I had been concentrating all of my energy into trying to give my son all that I could muster up. I had made my wishes secondary, not entirely as some selfless maternal act but also, as I could see retrospectively, as an excuse not to pursue, and potentially fail at, my own dreams. I had been rejoicing in my son's successes and claiming them as my own.

Maybe we all live through our children to some degree. Given the time and energy that we dedicate to raising our children, though, it is hardly surprising that the void that takes the place of their departure can feel a bit daunting. There are so many possibilities in life that we do not take advantage of because we are taken up with the daily ins and outs of child rearing and we tend to put ourselves on the back burner. All of a sudden, even though we have had years to think about it, we are faced with the gaping hole that our children have filled for so many years. We are faced with so many choices and it can feel too huge to contemplate. The finality of it all can ring like a physical and emotional shock and, as when coping with any shock, we need to be kind to ourselves.

It is a time to nurture ourselves and take life at whatever speed it feels right to live it at. If that means sitting in a darkened room for a couple of days wrapped in your child's dressing gown then so be it. If it means going out on the town and celebrating, then that is alright too. If you need to seek out company, then make sure it is the right company and not somebody who simply wants to jolly you out of your quagmire. It is a difficult time; and that needs acknowledging rather than being with someone who insists on cheering you up and you end up having to spend an evening of all smiles and laughter when you feel quite the opposite.

You may want to go back home and simply spend time on your own. You may want to put off the moment of going back home and being faced with the empty space that has for so many years been filled with your child.

When you go back home there is something very poignant about your child's bedroom, which means so much more than simply being a physical space or just another room in the house. This is where you have read them bedtime stories. This is the space that you have insisted on being tidied up for so long. This is where you have tiptoed in to make sure that they are safe and asleep. This is where you have crept in with a stocking full of surprises in the early hours of Christmas morning. This is also where your child's smell is and it is alright to bury your face in their pillow and weep.

One mum was amazed by her reaction of wanting to wear her

daughter's clothes to be able to get her smell. 'It's not as if she's died is it?' she had exclaimed, not being able to understand her own behaviour and seeing it as extreme to some extent. Maybe we spend too much time trying to apply logic to the situation when we could just accept that it is what it is. Accept whatever your reaction is and that this, also, is only temporary.

The immediate aftermath highlights the fact that everything you have been doing until now for the past however many years has revolved around your child or children. This is the very nature of being a parent and can feel as though your purpose in life has been removed. It takes a fair bit of getting used to, but it is not all tears and tissues.

The immediate aftermath is a hotch-potch of emotions that collide with each other as they meet one another coming back. Just as you are feeling overwhelmed with loneliness, end of life and purpose and 'who the hell am I now?' there is also a feeling of freedom and elation. Along with the loss there is also an element of liberation. A responsibility has been lifted. Responsibility is somehow equated with burden which is not necessarily the case. A child is not a burden but they are certainly a responsibility and a huge one at that. It is a responsibility that is mostly relished and treasured but that does not mean for a minute that it is not a relief to have that lifted.

The quiet house that you return to, as long as you do not have several more noisy children waiting in the wings, can have its upside. You can sit in silence. A silence that you have longed for. A silence that you have worked long and hard for. Much as the silence may feel deafening, ringing with the sound of loss, there may also be the sweet song of the future tinkling away quietly in the background.

It may be early days but this is a time when you can start thinking about all those things that you have always wanted to do. The things that you would dream of when you were unable to get out of the house, when you were knee-deep in nappies or homework. The immediate aftermath is also a good time to cash in on that extra adrenaline to get some jobs done in the house that you may have been meaning to do for ages but not had the time or the inclination for. There can be a surge of energy brought about by a life change and this can be put to good use. A lick of paint round the house and a good old sort out and tidy up.

Somehow there is a need to get things in order and make some sense of it all. Sometimes it feels as though there is a need to mark the change in the house with something more tangible like a different colour wall. Something that is a visible rather than something that is just being felt.

It is an idea to keep any changes in the immediate aftermath to a minimum. It can be unsettling for a child to come back home to complete change as though their parents have celebrated their departure with a house makeover. A total overhaul can leave a child feeling that they have been somewhat erased in their absence. I remember my dad turning my bedroom into a dark room to do photography. A good use of space actually, but there was a bit of me that felt ousted by the enlarging machine or whatever it was that took the place of the bed. But this is also a perfect example of how my dad was able to do something that he had always wanted to do and could now do with the extra time and space that my departure had created.

Even in the run up to departure when it can feel as though we are becoming redundant, just being present can be very time consuming.

To some extent, as parents, we are still living our lives around our children and not finding time for ourselves in those years. In amongst the sadness of their final departure it is time to sift through the tears and find the upside of the situation.

One of the first positive aspects of the immediate aftermath that many parents are quick to point out is that the loo rolls now seem to last forever. I have no idea why this should be so but it is true. Young people, for whatever reason — and this is not gender specific — seem to use up an inordinate amount of loo roll. There is also the fact that the fridge stays full of food. You are able to buy all the yummy food- stuff that you have long since wanted to buy without the fear of it disappearing while you lie innocently asleep. If you washed up the night before then in the morning the sink is still free of a stack of dirty plates and cups. In fact, the whole house is as you left it. It is nothing short of a miracle!

There is so much time to do so little in and you can wander peacefully from one room to the next without fear of demands and interruptions. You can take charge of the remote control. You can use the bathroom whenever you want. All the shampoo is there unused. There is a full tank of hot water and the plug is free of hair. The towels are unused and still folded and they are dry.

The phone stays silent and if it does ring you are not required to be a social secretary; although now that everybody has their own mobile phone the constant ringing of the house phone is rapidly becoming a thing of the past. In the few short years since my son has left home this is perhaps a frustration that has become no longer relevant.

If you have the house to yourself and can remember how, you can finally have noisy sex. Or you can just sit. You can sit some more and it does not get questioned. You can go back to the fridge because it is still full of the food that you bought. In fact, you can now eat what you want. It has been a long time and maybe you don't even remember what you used to like to eat but now is the time to start experimenting. Once you have got used to making meals with normal portion sizes, you realise that your meals are now your own to be had and enjoyed. Or you can eat cereal morning, noon and night for as long as you wish. You no longer have to set an example to anyone. You can do whatever you please and you can bask in your very own well-earned break.

One mum said that she skipped the tears altogether as she knows that her children are soon going to return. As sad as she felt, she was also determined to not mourn their departure but to enjoy the freedom that her children's departure had allowed her.

Another mum spoke of being delighted in the immediate aftermath and said 'I love it! I feel a bit guilty that I love it so much! Aren't I meant to feel even just a tiny bit sad?' She had recovered from her tears very quickly and went straight to enjoying the peace and quiet.

Not everyone is going to feel as though their insides are being turned upside down and that a limb is being gnawed off a little bit at a time and she settled into life without children like a comfy cardigan that she never wanted to take off. The novelty of waking up to all that space, freedom and unsullied tidiness never wore off. She had mild feelings of guilt but they were only fleeting and she did not think for one minute that she should feel any differently. She was able to relish every minute that she had the house to herself and was determined to take full advantage of it.

There was still a tinge of guilt, though, which is something that most parents know something about. Why does nobody warn you about the guilt when you become a parent? And why is there that very special guilt reserved just for parenthood? There are many things that will fuel the fires of parental guilt and one of those can be feeling delighted at having your own space to yourself. Ignore it if you can! Everyone is different, though, and so they should be. For some people the initial euphoria of the freedom will wear off and transform into sadness and loneliness, which can gallop in the wake of all that surface joy.

It can be hard to just go with whatever is happening and not be influenced by what we think we should or ought to be feeling, as the mum above pointed out, saying 'Aren't I meant to feel a tiny bit sad?' I do wonder how much of our reactions are tailored or curbed by society's view of how we should be reacting to the departure of our children and the loss of our role as parents. We are allowed to be a bit sad, but not too miserable as we are expected to be joyful that our children have found purpose in life and have flown the nest with all its restrictions and family-bound ties. And of course we are, but that does not mean that we cannot be sad at the same time. It is not as straightforward as simply being sad for us or happy for our children. Life, and parenthood in particular, is never that straightforward.

In the immediate aftermath people continually ask 'So what are you going to do now then?' I cannot begin to tell you how many people asked me that when my son had just left home. What is meant by that? Does it mean that your purpose is defined by the vicinity of your child? Does it mean that you are meant to go out and go wild?

Does it mean that you are meant to be at home mourning? Does it mean that you should be grabbing all of the opportunities out there and suddenly becoming superwoman?

Maybe it was just an innocent enquiring question but it made me feel that me without my child and simply doing what I was doing was not quite enough for some reason. It felt almost as though I had done what I was meant to do, breed and raise a child, and that now I had to justify my existence with something a bit more spectacular. Or that my son had been a restriction to me in some way and that I should now be off hurling myself towards some new and exotic destination. Actually I was just feeling a bit overwhelmed by it all.

It is not just us parents who are feeling overwhelmed at this time. Our children are having a pretty mammoth time of it as well. My son described his first experience of arriving in a different country on his own as that of being daunted by how big the world had just got. He said that it was like zooming out on Google maps and seeing how small he was. This passed after a few days and he said that it was like zooming back in again, just somewhere totally new. Although it was daunting initially, he quickly began to soak up his new surroundings like a sponge.

Another young person described the immediate aftermath as being a feeling of immense sadness descending on her as her mum left her. She suddenly felt quite small and out of her depth but quickly realised that there were many people in the same situation as her and people that she could talk to who would be able to understand. She soon began to enjoy her new surroundings and relished being somewhere new with so much to learn.

It would seem that children are going through a similar pattern to their parents when they leave home except that it is perhaps a bit diluted as it is their choice and they are at the more optimistic end of life. Many young people have spoken of that initial feeling of the enormity of being without the safety and familiarity of home which is soon overtaken by excitement at their new situation and the potential out there in the world and in them.

Young people are going out into the world to start new ventures, as is only right. As parents, we might be at home doing the same thing but nothing is the same. It might be that you have other children at home who still need looking after and so life carries on. It carries on in a different way but the immediate day-to-day role of being a parent has not been removed. It may be that different things are high-lighted in the relationships with the other children. It may be that remaining children have to jiggle their relationships about as one person is taken out of the equation.

One young person described the calm that descended on their house once one of the siblings had left home and said there was also a bit of guilt that they all felt so much happier without the departed sibling there. Another young person described the void left by her sister and said that she really did not know how to communicate properly with her parents once her sister was not there. She realised that she had communicated largely with and via her sister. She also felt alienated from her sister as it was the first time that her sister was out having experiences of which she was not a part.

Parents may feel resentful that they are not given the space by the remaining children to be able to grieve for the child that has left home. A parent might just need a bit of time to themselves but is taken up with dealing with the potential upset of the other children as they are also getting used to a sibling leaving and the hole that this leaves in the family. A parent might feel that their role has changed. It has been shuffled about, as have the dynamics of the remaining family members. It has been changed but it has not been taken away. It may not make it any easier to have children at home but it is different.

With one child the parenting experience comes to an abrupt halt. There is no gentle easing into the empty nest by one child leaving and then it being some years later before the last one goes and by then it is quite likely that some of the others have come back again! With one child you are a being a parent one day, in the active sense, and then not being a parent the next day. With one child, the empty nest event is definite and there is no slow introduction into a world where your primary role is not that of parent. The waving off at the train station, university, airport or wherever it may be, is the final gesture and adieu to the parenting experience, as you have always known it. One day you have lots of washing to do and the next day you do not. One day you are constantly filling up the fridge and the next day you are not. One day you have someone with whom your daily life is connected and the next day you are set adrift. The change is stark and very noticeable.

Everyone will tell you that you never stop being a parent and of course this is true. But you do stop being a parent in its current form and performing all of the daily parent tasks. There is a marked change in what was once some kind of routine. It may be that the routine had become increasingly diluted as your child became more independent within the family home but it is a routine nonetheless.

A young person who is leaving home and leaving siblings behind may face living on their own, or being on their own in a bedroom, for the first time. Delightful some might say: one young person spoke of how brilliant it was to finally get a bedroom to herself and not have to live with somebody else's mess. Her sister, left behind, found it hard to sleep, though. She also found that life in the family changed considerably with her sister no longer there. The dynamics of remaining family members had to shift in order to accommodate the change brought about by the one family member leaving.

One mum spoke of her daughter missing her sister who had left home to go to university. She also said that it had become obvious that, as a mum, she had spent far more time with the daughter who had left. She had to spend time to repair what she hadn't realised was a flawed relationship with her younger daughter. She also felt guilty when she spoke about missing her daughter who had left home and the fact that she actually enjoyed spending time with her more as, with similar personalities, they got on better.

One young person who is the eldest of several siblings spoke of being very excited at leaving the family home and no longer feeling responsible for her younger brothers and sisters. She was excited about finding a whole new life for herself without the rest of the family. Being part of a big family can become a strong part of a young person's identity and they may struggle to see themselves as someone functioning on their own initially.

I have two older brothers and I remember that when I left home I was delighted at the novelty of being able to spend time with other girls and to learn to live with other females. Finally there were people who would actually speak to me and would want to just spend the evening chatting away over nothing in particular!

It may be that couples are faced, for the first time in many years, with spending time on their own together. A dear friend of mine has no children of her own but has spent thirty years looking after, and working with, a large number of children and families. She has been a part of many families that have grown and changed with children leaving home. She has spoken of seeing parents lose themselves in their children. She has seen that, often, everything that parents do is for or with their children and that they forget to think about themselves and their relationship. She said that she wishes parents would allow their children more freedom by having a life independent of them. She has seen many parents surprised by the shock and grief that they feel and experience when their children leave home.

She has also seen many relationships fail once the children leave home as they acted as the glue keeping the parents together. Parents have also spoken to her about them staying together 'for the sake of the children'. She was able to offer valuable insight from the perspective of someone who has not been a parent but has been deeply involved and such an integral part of so many families. She has been a great support to young people who have left home and do not feel able to talk to their parents about the problems that they may be experiencing.

The flip side of that is that parents may rejoice in finally finding themselves on their own and research bears out that many couples experience a great deal of improvement in the quality of their relationship once children leave home and that they get to spend more time together. My parents spent time going out for dinner which is something that they could not previously do with several children at home. They had more money and more time to spend that money in.

Statistics show that an average family is about £600 a month better off once their children leave home. I do wonder whether this is as valid a statistic since the onset of increased university fees and increasing costs of living in general. I would assume that many parents now find themselves struggling just as much, if not more, while their children are at university.

My parents, though, found that in the immediate aftermath they were better off in many ways and they basked in the euphoria of their new-found freedom. This did not last long, however, as they slipped back into their routines and the novelty began to wear off. This is something that many parents have spoken about, that actually it is when the novelty and euphoria wears off that they begin to struggle with their new situation.

The immediate aftermath is usually the time when sympathy is meted out to parents experiencing their first taste of an empty nest, and straight away certainly, this is much needed. But actually this can also be the time when, as a parent, you are feeling most elated and pumped up by your fantastic achievement of having raised an independent and fully functioning (hopefully) person and released them into the world. This is generally not when the real rock-solid support is needed. That comes later on, as the jubilation at having reached some sort of parental goal mutates and transforms itself into something a little less clear and far more deep-rooted.

The immediate aftermath is characterised by swooping highs and lows that are unsettling and do not always feel easy to manage. But this rollercoaster then settles into something else after a little bit of time has gone by.

CHAPTER 3

AFTER A LITTLE BIT OF TIME
HAS GONE BY

Time moves on. Times takes on a strange pace as you start to adjust to life without your child. As with all experiences of loss, it is almost as if time is speeding up and slowing down all at the same time. This does also, of course, depend on how many children you have left at home who are keeping you in the routine of being a parent. But let us take the instance of this being your only or last child that has left home.

There comes a time, after a little bit of time has gone by, when a sense of emptiness starts to settle upon the house. Where there was once movement and noise there is now quiet. Even where there are children left in the home, still creating family chaos, there is going to be a void left by the departed sibling. The initial euphoria and business of preparing a child for departure, and then getting used to them having gone, has worn off and something else has moved into its place. Except that it is difficult to know what that something else is.

The previous life of routine that involved school timetables, shopping for loads of food and giving lifts, to here there and everywhere, starts to fade. The constant presence of a person who, potentially, is about to make demands of some kind or other, even if just upon your time, is something that is no longer. It starts to become something that was and will never be again and the reality of it all begins to sink in.

This is a difficult time and friends may need reminding that you are still undergoing a time of adjustment. Friends who may have been there at the beginning, when the immediate departure of your child felt raw, may forget that you are actually still trying to get used to something pretty big. While they may have easily taken in your new status of empty nest, for you it takes a little bit longer. It takes more than a couple of weeks to undo the habits and lifestyle that you have been living for the past 18 years or more.

There begins a sense of the forever after. It is a taste of what is to be in the future, and ahead looms a life without the daily input and reassurance of a child to confirm your parental status. There are constant triggers in your daily life to remind you of the enormity of what is happening. Apart from the excess of loo rolls and lack of empty milk bottles which remains a source of joy and wonder, there are other factors that remind you of the holes now in your life.

One mum spoke about how difficult she found it to cater for fewer people in the house. Her husband eventually commented on the huge portions of food at each meal time and this was enough to bring on another wave of sadness for her. This is the time when you might hear parents talking about their children non-stop and it is easy to forget that not everybody is as interested in your child's new life as you are. Simply talking about them can feel as though it is keeping them in your life and that you are still as involved as you have always been. But this is not true.

It takes time to inch away from the daily parenting that was. It is almost as if this is the in-between zone — between being a busy parent and moving on to the next step — and the will to hang on to the previous life can come over in huge waves. We cling to the title of busy parent until we feel brave enough to take a leap towards the next bit of life.

It is at this point that, as parents, we are starting to poke our heads out of the parental cave to see what is out there in the big world. We cannot remember life as it was pre-children because nothing is the same any more. But there comes a point when stick our heads out we must and test what life has to offer, however tempting it might be just to hide. After the initial taste of a child-free life, a mild exhaustion takes over before you can feel ready to move onwards and upwards. The initial euphoria of freedom and lack of structure that the immediate aftermath was able to offer was just a phase and now further bravery is called for. It is time to move forwards and take life by the proverbial horns despite all instincts that may be crying out to the contrary.

As the novelty of the freedom starts to wear off after a little bit of time has gone by, you might find yourself hankering for the loud music and piles of washing that were once the bane of your day. All of those things that used to be so irritating and a prime source of complaint can start to take on a rosy hue. It is almost as if the hustle and bustle of family life that was has taken on a different memory form even in such a short time. It can be easy to look back and forget the times when you felt like tearing your hair out and just remember it as all sweetness and light.

I remember my mum talking about Sundays being her favourite day of the week, when all of the family would come together for a roast dinner. My memories are that of wishing that I could be out spending time with my friends. Although, mum's roast potatoes were always a draw to the family hearth! I can see now that what she remembers is the family time and the status of being a mum. She remembers a time when things were clear, including her role in life. It can be hard to face a future where that role that we have taken on with such dedication is no longer, or at least not in the familiar shape that it has always been. We can start to look back at those times and the people in them in a different light and perhaps imagine a reality different from that which actually happened.

As with grief there can be a certain status of reverence that is awarded to the departed. It is almost as if talking about them, and remembering them, in only a positive way will help to keep them close. You look back at the things that made you scream from the inside out and they now make you chuckle fondly. All of those things that people promised you that you would be able to look back on and laugh at are now laughable. The late nights, the classic incidents that then, in time, become family stories that are dragged out at opportune and inopportune moments. Stories of being drunk, being caught smoking, the first girlfriend/boyfriend, and all those occasions that were hugely irritating at the time, now become fond memories.

All of those times that you fed loads of hungry teenagers and you longed for a peaceful evening watching your very own television programme of choice without being invaded. Well, now you have your wish granted and this reality stretches ahead of you like a barren wasteland waiting to swallow you up in its silence. How could you have ever thought that providing endless fodder was anything other than a deep joy?

The truth is that you begin to miss it all. From now on the clocks are only going to march forwards and all of those child-rearing years have been lost and gone, many of them swallowed up in a hurry to get through it all.

It is not just parents who start to struggle after a little bit of time has gone by. My son spoke of missing home after a couple of months of being away. He said that once a routine had been established, and the novelty of leaving home had worn off slightly, he found himself in a weird no-man's land. He was happy about being somewhere else but had not been away long enough to feel at home where he was and started to feel a bit homesick. He remembers the weekends being particularly difficult as they were empty compared with the busy, organised week days and that this left a gap.

Another young person spoke of the weekends being a time when she wished she was at home and that this was when she found it the most difficult. The excitement of meeting new people had tempered slightly and she just felt tired. She also said that after a couple of months was when she saw other people struggling and wanting to go home. After a little bit of time has gone by it would seem that everybody would like just a little pause for things to go back to how they were and then get on with their lives again. But the clocks cannot turn back and life has changed.

Life starts to settle in to a new way of being and as one mum said 'I feel as if I am losing touch with them'. For the first time ever your child is leading a life of which you know little about and of which you play practically no part. This is no bad thing but it just takes some getting used to. For the first time there is a need to form a new relationship with your child that is not based upon the daily routine of home. Previously, whether we liked it or not, there was a relationship that involved coordinating lifestyles to some degree. Will you be home for tea? Are you coming back tonight? Do you need the car? All of the everyday things that keep us all ticking over without us even realising it. Once a child has left home we are no longer inextricably linked with them purely on the basis of living under the same roof.

After a little bit of time has gone by, an effort needs to be made to keep in touch but there rears the question — how much do you keep in touch? Is every day too much? Probably. There again everybody is different and it depends how involved you were in one another's lives before your child left home. I do wonder how the changing face of technology and the continuous ways of being in touch change the way in which young people are able to distance themselves from the family home. Once upon a time, no news was good news and it was rare that a child would contact home once they had left. The occasional letter or phone call either to ask for money, a flight back home, a food parcel or simply to reassure home that you were still alive was enough to satisfy parents.

Now it is so much easier to be in contact that there has to be a good reason for several days or weeks to go by without any updates. I am not sure whether this makes it easier or harder for young people to settle into their new lives. There can be the danger of a child being able to contact home every time something feels uncomfortable in their new lives. In some respects this is no bad thing but it can also mean that a child never gets to work things out for themselves without their parents acting as a prop allowing them to go forth into the world.

This also leaves parents being updated regularly regarding the ups and downs of their child's life. Any young person who has just left home is bound to have many ups and downs even in the space of just one day. The very transient nature of youth means that this can pass within hours. As parents we are left feeling dreadful when we hear news of how terrible life is for our child if they tell us about it. Having vented their frustrations they may immediately be feeling better while we are left biting our nails until the next contact that will have, hopefully, a more optimistic outlook.

When we live in the same house as our children those moments of angst are mixed with more temperate activities, such as maybe just watching the television. They come and go in waves. We see our children feeling miserable but in the next breath we see them chatting with a friend. It is easier to be able to dismiss what may be the small stuff. When we live in separate homes those moments of angst are concentrated into one phone call, undiluted by any other daily activities that may be peppered with laughter and other conversation. The mere question of geography means we cannot possibly be there for every problem that arises and there comes a time when we, and our children, just have to get used to that. It is only right that it should be that way. They are out there seeing the world and have to work it out for themselves at some stage or other.

Young people now have different complications to deal with when they leave home. It is true that every generation will have some similarities and there will always be differences. It may always have been the case that, on leaving home, there is a feeling that you should be conquering the world but do not know quite where to begin. Now, though, young people have access to far more information than was ever available in previous generations.

When I left home I knew that I didn't have a clue about what was going on in the world. I wonder whether continual internet access from a young age has given this current generation a false sense of knowing about the world. In one sense they are better equipped with more information about where they are going and what they want to be doing and this can only be a positive. In another sense, even though a young person is now able to find out pretty much anything at the press of a button, getting out there into the big wide world is very different. All of the information available cannot prepare them for the actual reality of this.

The plus side is that moving out of familiar home ground, leaving home to go to university, work or travelling can personalise what is read about on the internet or in books. Even if the move from home just takes a child round the corner minutes from the family, it is able to make real what has only been imagined up until now. Technology allows young people to plan in a way that was never possible before, have choices and also to share with others what is happening in their new world.

It is wonderful to hear your child talk about what they have experienced in person outside of the comfort of the family home and it is a delight to see their world getting bigger with each day. One mum said how proud she was of her son, that she had seen a whole new side to him and that she was really proud of the way that he had managed any obstacles that he had encountered.

As it was exciting in the lead up to departure when getting involved in your child's plans for the future, so now it is exciting to hear about what they are making of their world and how their horizons are expanding. It can be inspiring to hear how they have overcome any difficulties and reached conclusions about the new life that is now surrounding them.

Young people, when they first leave home, have to learn to live with a whole new bunch of people that are not their family and I am continually amazed about how they manage to do this. Generally, when a person first leaves home, they do not have the luxury of their own place to live in. Often they will be sharing their living space with other people that, usually, they have never met before. This requires a degree of negotiating skills that is immense. That and tolerance towards new housemates. It is often the first time that a young person has had to share a bathroom and kitchen with people who are not family or friends and is not, at least at first, allowed to shout at those with whom they are sharing when they get on their nerves. At home, most yelling matches are forgiven within the space of a day but they do not yet know how their housemates might react. Besides, when you first meet people there is a general will for every-one to display their best traits and leave the screaming until they have got to know one another a bit better. Most people quite like to portray themselves as pleasant people, at least initially.

They start to learn how other people live and introduce that into their own lives (and then bring that home again — but more of that later!). They learn to compromise around problems that may never have arisen in their lives before and I have been in awe of some of the young people that I have heard speak about their house-sharing experiences. A young person may be leaving home for the first time to move in with their partner and having to learn a whole new lifestyle to gel with their own.

They start to learn to budget their own money, or not, as the case may be. And herein lies one of the big parental dilemmas. For how long do we keep bailing out our children financially? What are the limits? And when do those limits change and under what circumstances? I have been very fortunate with my son in that he has never made massive demands or needed bailing out. There have been a few sticky patches but nothing totally unmanageable.

But I do know many families where this is not the case. What do you do when your child says that they have no money for food and yet you know that they have been out partying and blown their budget on drink or whatever else? At what point does that stop being our responsibility? I can imagine that there never comes a point in life when it gets any easier to watch your own child struggling financially if you have the means to help them out. This does not make it right or any less complicated.

Some people, for whatever reason, find it much harder than others to be able to manage their money realistically. Some people find it practically impossible. It is never less than frustrating and can be an infinite source of conflict between parent and child. If the parents take control and limit their budget in some way, does this hinder their ability to ever work it out for themselves? Or does it offer the strict boundaries and reality check that is needed? It might be worth having a money conversation with your child before they leave home and establishing what you are prepared, and not prepared, to do in the face of a financial shortfall on their part.

It is worth going through in some detail what it costs on a daily basis to keep body and soul in roughly the same time zone. It is worth the raised eyebrows and sarcastic responses elicited when you go through the consequences of blowing a possibly restricted budget in the first few weeks of having left home. No matter how much is budgeted, life generally costs a bit more than that. It is not always a question of how children are raised and educated about money because you can have children from the same family and one child will 'get it' and another child will most definitely not.

Although I do not have the answers, I do have enough experience of seeing various families struggle with this issue to know that it is worth giving it a great deal of consideration. Obviously different families have different attitudes to money and what it signifies for them. There is also the issue of the need to be needed on the part of the parents and money plays quite a big part in that. Money can become a form of currency in more than the financial sense of the word and can become a bartering for affection. An easy trap to fall into and it is well to be forewarned as much as is humanly possible.

Apart from the fact that your child is at a stage in life when being able to manage their own money is a pretty useful skill to have, there is also the fact that you could be spending that money. There is all that money that was once spent on supplying copious amounts of loo roll that is now gathering a small fortune! After a little bit of time has gone by it starts to occur to parents that they could, in fact, be going out themselves and having a nice time spending the money that their child seems so happy to fritter away.

It takes a little while once your child has left home for it to sink in that all that spare time that seems to stretch ahead, that felt daunting and empty, could actually be filled with something fun or constructive. You are starting to make that final adjustment to the changes that have been brought about in the family home and it can be an ideal time to take a good long look at ourselves. It is not easy.

As a parent we spend so long thinking about other people and dashing about making things happen, making lists, getting to places on time and cajoling reluctant offspring into carrying out daily tasks, that we can forget about what we might actually want out of our day. This is an ideal time to start letting go of daily obligations and to start thinking about possibilities for the future. Who knows what lies around the corner? There is spare time to be had. In theory there is some spare money to be had. Technically there should be some extra head space to be had. This is easier said than done. Parents spend years thinking about who they should be and who they actually are in relation to their children. There can be a massive gap between who we think we should be and who we actually believe that we are. If we do not start to let go of all the 'should be' thoughts then we might miss what is potentially round the corner.

This is not just a time for children to fly the nest but a time for parents to dust off old thoughts and dreams that may have been lying dormant in the attics of our minds for years. After a little bit of time has gone by, and the feeling of yesteryear being the golden age has settled under your skin and been incorporated well and truly into your new state of being, then a new page starts to open up.

One mum spoke very honestly of looking back at the years of frustration while bringing up her two boys. She talked of having got stressed at trying to set them out on a world-wide adventure until she realised that her need to keep enquiring after their welfare was greater than theirs and that they were surviving perfectly well without her. She found herself asking how it had all happened so quickly and how they get to be all grown up all of a sudden. But then she saw that a new life was opening up to her once she had got used to the reality that her sons would be joined to her life in a different way. She started to see what she could do with the second half of her life that lay before her and suddenly life did not seem so bleak after all. In fact, it was looking to be a whole load of fun.

It is human nature to be able to adapt to whatever circumstances we find ourselves living in — otherwise we would quickly go a little bit off centre. It is also human nature to be generally optimistic about our circumstances and to try and better our lives in whatever way we can, otherwise humankind would quickly grind to a halt. However much a person may pride themselves on being eternally miserable, even the most miserable person will try and find something that might make them feel slightly buoyant even if only for an instant. After the initial shock of being exposed to the world without a child to buffer you against the winds of change, you can start to straighten youself up and look at the world through different eyes. You can start to adapt and find the positives — and there are many — of the situation.

As parents we need retraining in the art of how to carry on conversations that are not framed around term times, schoolwork and various activities that our children take part in. We need retraining in how to think only for ourselves right the way through the day. After a little bit of time has gone by the restless pacing around the house can be replaced by something a little more resigned, but also something a little more territorial. Maybe it is time to reclaim your space — both mental and physical. You can start to make friends with yourself all over again and notice bits of your old self that begin to emerge from their long hibernation. The bits that were squashed or hidden by the eternal quest for domestic cooperation and harmony. There is now peace and quiet given over to your uninterrupted thoughts.

In your newfound peaceful surroundings, you can start to build a sense of logic around your situation. There is life beyond children leaving home. Of course there are still moments of sadness and of course you always worry for their welfare and safety but crikey it does feel good to stretch yourself around the house as you see fit. You start to sift through advertisements for courses or classes on things that you had long given up hope of ever being able to do. You start saying yes to any invitations that might come your way. In fact, you could get used to this.

Just as you have got into the swing of doing pretty much just as you please, your child starts to make noises of wanting to return home. As a general point of reference this is usually after about six months. This is not an exact science but it does seem to be the length of time it takes for someone to leave home, have a brilliant time and then to start missing home and winding their way back again.

Children that have left to go to university are provided with their own punctuation marks of when to return home. This is fairly clearly laid out before they leave home when they are given a timetable. University has become a relatively standard way for young people to leave home and it is a fairly gentle easing into the empty nest situation for parents. For young people it may be easier for them to gauge how they manage leaving home given that there are term times with natural breaks when they can come home.

There is also the onset of the gap year, which has also become a way of leaving home and seeing the world. One young person said about her gap year travels that she struggled to stay away for the whole year and would have been happy to come home earlier but she that was with two friends who were determined to stay away for the whole eight months planned. She felt that she was ready to come home after six months and luxuriate in the home comforts that she remembered so fondly.

As different as every situation is every person, who may or may not miss home, and may or may not want to return home. But come home they do! Just when you have settled into the idea of having reclaimed your own space. Just when the gaps between the tears and the euphoria have lengthened and possibly even abated altogether. Just when you have started not to think about your child every minute of every day and have managed to carve out chunks of your day that belong entirely to you. Just when you are really starting to enjoy this new life of doing what you like when you like. Just when it seems that you have established some sort of different relationship with your child that encompasses time doing your own thing. Just when all of this is settling into something of its very own shape, your offspring decide to bounce back and you realise that it is all going to change again.

CHAPTER 4

THEN THEY'RE BACK AGAIN

So you have got into the swing of eating what you want and when you want to. You have retrained yourself to be 'selfish' and nurture those long lost needs whatever they may be. For the first time in your life, or for a very long time, you do not have to explain yourself to anyone or be an example to anyone and it is starting to feel mighty comfortable. Then you get the phone call... They are coming home!

And boy, are they back again! Mixed feelings course their way through your heart and body. Deep joy that your child is winding their way back home and you cannot wait to see them again. It has been as long as you are able to go without seeing them and the parental heartstrings have been stretched to their full capacity before they actually snap. At long last you will be able to give them a massive hug and take care of them once again. You can hear of their adventures (or those that you want to hear about anyway) and reuniting will be exciting and wonderful. You are looking forward to seeing your child in their new grown up skin and finding out what new methods of reasoning on life they have adopted.

Hot on the heels of your delight comes a niggling worry and a bit of you is wondering if you are going to have to relinquish any of your new found liberty or whether you can all come to a whole new agreement. You push these thoughts to one side as you nervously wait at arrivals at the airport/station/high street/front door. You hop from one foot to the other, unable to get on with anything else until their appearance has been made, until you have finally made contact. You have been talking about 'the day' with friends since you received the phone call telling of their arrival or the day that had been planned since their departure if you have a more organised child and family. You are trying to picture them in all their newness. Will they have changed?

Generally a child who has left home for the first time and has then come back again is full of their first exposure to the world. They are no longer the sum total of all that has happened within the family home and environment. Most children are happy to be home; it is somewhere that they have thought about and talked about while they were away. From being somewhere that they were once keen to get away from, in their absence home has often been built up into something fantastic and ideal.

It is easy to idealise what has been left behind when they are feeling a bit homesick and not quite sure about the world or at least the little bit of world that they have found themselves in. Home is a point of reference to which they are able to compare all of their experiences while they have been away. Often there is nothing quite like their own bed, their own pillows and the comfort of the family sofa. A lot of children claim that their mum's home cooking is the best in the world and there is always something that makes a certain aspect of home stand out from anything else that has been encountered. It is generally good to be home again and it has felt like a long slog to get there whether it be by plane, train or automobile.

Home is gloriously familiar but there is now somehow something missing. There are all the comforts of home and the knowledge that there is a well carved out space which they can slip back into. There is the sanctuary of their own bedroom space (presuming it is still there) that contains all of their history and can be an anchor point in time. A reference to simpler times in life before they had launched themselves for their initial flight from the nest. There is often a new appreciation of all that is done in the home, and something as simple as doing the washing is now received with a whole new level of gratitude. It might even be that when they are back again they start to help out around the house a bit more. Our children have had their first taste of doing things for themselves and can maybe now see that it is not all as simple as it first seems. Things do not 'just appear' before their eyes but require planning, budgeting and all the rest that goes with running a household. It might be that they are not quite at the stage where they think that this applies to you and your household but they are certainly taking their first steps towards this being the case.

Initially things are pretty delightful. In fact the joy of seeing your child for the first time again is something that is unrivalled. One mum described it beautifully after having seen her daughter for the first time since leaving to go to university. She described breathing as being something that is instinctive, not something that we give much thought to throughout the day. When she saw her daughter she described the joy and smiles that filled her as being similar to breathing. Something that she had no choice but to feel and that it was a totally natural thing to happen.

It is not until you are actually able to hold your child and physically witness their well-being that you realise that a part of you had been on complete tenterhooks the whole time that they had been away. Another mum spoke of the time that her daughter had returned after a year travelling abroad. She said that she kept following her daughter round the house and poking her to make sure that she was real! Once the novelty and humour of this had worn off for the daughter, the mum was quickly encouraged to stop doing this!

However much technology has allowed us to be in regular contact with our children and to continually reassure ourselves of their well-being there is nothing quite like real life physical contact. It is immensely joyful to feel, if only for a short time, that everything is back as it should be. Everyone is back in their natural and rightful place and we can all relax into how things have always been.

Except we cannot do that. Things are not as they have always been, something has fundamentally changed. There has been a definite shift in the dynamics of the relationship between parent and child while they have been away from home and now it all needs to be rejiggled into its new-found place. There is the joy of familiarity on both parts that is also tinged with the knowledge that something has changed irreversibly. This is like stepping into a new territory in the parenting world. One that takes a whole new level of negotiation and rethinking.

It can be helpful to be quite clear about establishing the differences that have come about during your time apart. One young person that I spoke to said that he found it helpful to know where he stood, when his mum sat him down to talk about the rules in the house, on his return home. This may not suit everyone but they obviously knew what worked for them. Siblings that have remained at home may have established relationships between themselves while the other sibling has been away from home and there runs the risk of someone feeling excluded somewhere along the line. The returning sibling may disrupt, or feel that they have disrupted, the balance of what has been established in their absence. Old patterns in the family may be returned to or the returning sibling may not know where they fit in.

Another young person that I spoke to said that she is the eldest of several siblings and that she was the first to leave home. Due to the age gap between her and the younger children at home she feels that she has missed out on their essential growing up years, especially the adolescent years. She spoke of the other siblings all having a bond as a group through the experiences of those years but that she feels out on a limb and not actually part of the 'gang'. She has managed to establish a relationship with each sibling on an individual basis but not with them all as a whole. Being the first to leave home has, for her, been a slightly isolating experience.

It is said that the relationship between siblings is the one that is the longest lasting throughout any person's lifetime and yet I wonder how much consideration is given by parents to the long term outcome of sibling relationships. I wonder how much energy is focused on the daily task of raising them rather than allowing them the space to form a bond independently. There is a fine line to be struck between supervising siblings while also allowing their relationship to evolve.

In our family, rivalry was not discouraged and this bred a sense of injustice among us siblings that was hard to shake off even throughout adult years. But rather than feel distanced once I had left home I felt able to establish relationships with my siblings independently and got to know them in a different light.

This is a time when siblings start to live independently of one another and it takes dedication to maintain that relationship in its evolving form. It can be a time for them to get to know one another through their now separate worlds without the added dynamics of having to live under the same roof and vie for the attention of parents. I have seen siblings be the source of the most incredible support to one another and also the source of great heartache. They can be the greatest ally or the one who has access to knowing what presses all of the buttons of their sibling to be able to wind them up and disrupt their progress.

As a parent it becomes a time to begin to step back from their interactions and allow the relationship between siblings to mature rather than remain stuck as young children relying upon a parent's intervention to sort out differences.

For siblings this is also notoriously a time when a younger sibling will proudly announce to the departed sibling that they have taken over their bedroom. A sure sign of being promoted within the family home. An outward declaration that things have changed and that new territories have been marked out. When a child returns home they have to squeeze themselves back into a space that has been filled in their absence, as is only natural. But this can leave a child who leaves home and then returns feeling as though they have missed out on something a bit fundamental that they cannot quite put their finger on. They may feel that they are a bit of an outsider until the dynamics in the family have changed to incorporate them back into the fold.

With all the familiarity in the world it is possible to feel like a stranger, even if just for a little while. With the advent of increasing communication this may not be quite as much the case as it may have been in previous generations. With all the zillions of ways that there are to keep in touch it also means that a child will be updated and able to feel involved in any changes in the family home as they happen.

There is another side to the advent of technology that changes the way that young people are able to declare their return to the family home. On a very basic level any change in physical appearance is not the surprise that it once was. Any new haircuts/clothes/image can soon be delivered in an instant photo. In years not that far gone by (to me anyway) a child would appear back at the family hearth to cries of 'Oh your hair has grown/been all cut off/is pink!' and 'Oh you've lost weight/put on a bit/changed shape!'. All the tales of where a child had been and with whom would be reliant upon description or, if you were lucky, the odd scraggy photo that had survived several months in a backpack or being kicked around an overfilled room somewhere. Now photos can be uploaded, sent and dished out from the other side of the world at the press of a button. It can feel as though there is no place left to hide and that there is not the time for a young person to adjust to their own changes before those changes are known to their nearest and dearest.

This does change the return of children to the home as you may have been updated as the months have gone by and there may be little left to describe to one another. Despite there having been a great change on both sides, but more on the part of the young person, there may not be the time and space dedicated to them being able to regale all with their tales. Many of those tales may have already been told over the airwaves and with regularity. So this just leaves everyone to settle back in together.

When a child comes back home there may be a conflict of emotions of all sides. A young person is happy to be back home but is also missing what they have left and the new people that they have met in their new life. They may feel displaced and struggle to settle. I can remember that feeling really clearly — of coming back home and feeling very restless, as though the house had somehow shrunk. That I no longer really belonged there but that I didn't particularly belong anywhere else either. Other young people have also talked about the feeling of restlessness and that they were pacing around the house on their return not entirely sure of what to do.

During their time away from home a young person has had experiences and made friendships of which you, and the rest of the family, are no longer a part. They may share what they have been doing but it is very different from having been a part of the same household which is what the parent-child relationship has been based upon up until that time. It is like stepping into a whole new territory in the parenting world. Hopefully this is the basis for the relationship taking its first tentative steps towards functioning on a more equal footing rather than the one based upon the parent being the authority until that point. This takes hard work even though it is seemingly a most natural progression.

When a child first comes back home again there is the natural joy at seeing them once more. There is the natural slotting into place and feeling as though you have your role as parent back once more. But it is not just with the child that something has changed. As a parent you have had the first taste in many years of being able to do what you want without having to think of anybody else. It takes a bit of getting used to but once you get a flavour of it, life can be quite delicious.

All of sudden the whole situation is reversed but it is difficult to backtrack suddenly to a time when you had to prioritise your child within the home. The spare time that seemed to gape at you with expectant eyes during the immediate aftermath has since become filled with leisure or extra work or just thinking for yourself. Your pace of life has changed and that now has to change again. It can be hard, at times, not to feel resentful. The more a parent clutches at opportunities to snatch back time for themselves so a child, at whatever age, will try and invade that time and space.

As people when they retire often exclaim that they do not know how they ever found the time to work, so a parent, once-empty nested, might exclaim that they do not know how they ever found the time to be a parent! Your child may be making demands upon your time that you are no longer used to and having needs that you are no longer accustomed to meeting. It is the beginning of a child recognising that their parent is a person in their own right. Hopefully this has happened way before then but it can take quite a few years to sink in properly. Therein lies the conflict. On the one hand it does feel wonderful to see your child and to slip back into the role of parent like a pair of comfy slippers but on the other hand there can be a sense of intrusion into a new-found way of life.

On a very basic level there are the financial implications. Almost inevitably when your child returns to the family home they have no money, no job, no idea of what to do next and may not be generally happy with their situation. This is not always the case and there is the ever increasing scenario of a child that has left to go to university and comes back home during the term holidays. In which case they may be quite clear about what they are going to do next but they will still probably have no money.

It is hard to watch them rattling around the house wishing that they were elsewhere so you offer to give them lifts to places to save them bus and train fares. You suggest that friends come back to the house so that they do not have to spend money on going out. The house starts to fill up with a familiar noise of people which is initially wonderful. It can soon start to wear thin as you remember how you hardly ever got to watch your favourite film. The washing machine is doing its umpteenth wash. In the space of a day the fridge starts doing its emptying trick again and all of the loo rolls are used up overnight. The sink fills up again with dirty dishes and the mess is no longer your own.

When your child comes home you will be amazed at the amount of 'stuff' that they bring with them. It would seem that most young people have an unrealistic notion of what can be crammed into a car. I have heard many parents exclaim how they pack the car to the hilt when they pick up their children at the end of each university term. I have not had the experience of picking up a child's belongings from university but I have picked my son up many times from airports when he has brought home far more than the amount that he set out with.

Then all of that stuff, whether it be pots and pans from university, reams of useful paraphernalia gathered on travels or wherever they have been, comes into the house. What seems to fit happily into one box takes up far more than one box worth of space when it is on the outside of its box. Their possessions seem to spill over into all corners of the house. It may be that this is irritating because you have got used to having your own mess about. You have been revelling in the fact that you have not been having to nag anybody else about their mess or having to clean it up yourself while they have been away. They have travelled and they have gathered and it stands to reason that they would have more stuff than they left home with and that they have, until further notice, nowhere else to put it.

You can feel yourself returning to the nagging self that you thought you had waved goodbye to and you can feel your petrol tank of tolerance slowly emptying. None of this has anything to do with how much you love your child. It is possible to love somebody to the very ends of the earth but for them to still be intensely irritating.

While your child is away from home, geography does a great deal to dilute the angst that can accompany daily life. As a rule you may get told of the situations that are causing more concern rather than the daily niggles. It is unlikely, but not unheard of, that a child will phone to ask 'where are my socks?' which is something that can happen fairly regularly within the home. A child while they are away from home may talk to their parent about their housemates, the difficulty of being where they are being but, generally, they are not concerns that require an immediate response that might impact upon what you are doing and upon your time. By the time any misery arrives to you over the seas, through the time zones, down the halls of university or across the location of choice, it will often have taken on a different dimension and level of intensity both on the part of the recipient and the dealer of the news.

While back under the same roof the things of daily life can add up to be huge irritations. A simple request of 'where are my socks?' can easily lead to something bigger such as 'where you left them/on the floor/try looking for them/if you did the washing you would know/they are not your socks they are mine' etc, and so on. This may have been a daily dynamic that everybody was used to before your child's departure but you have now got used to not having those conversations and as they were irritating before, now they can become infuriating. The trick is to not let these seemingly minor things escalate into anything bigger. When things are said they cannot be unsaid. It takes restraint and patience. This was something that you used to have in truckloads but it seems to have dissipated somewhat in their absence.

Maybe tolerance is like a muscle and the less you use it, the less you are able to use it? Maybe there is a finite amount of tolerance to be used up in any one lifetime. An exhaustive pot of tolerance that is dipped into regularly while they are growing up but then you have to reach right to the bottom as the levels run out. Maybe running out of parental tolerance is one of the natural ways of children and parents distancing themselves from the parent-child dynamic that has always been.

I remember watching a mare and foal many years ago and the mare was kicking the foal away. At the time I thought how cruel this was but could, many years later, see that this was nature's way of telling the little one to get on with things on his own and that the mum just wanted to get on and eat some grass without being hassled for milk all the time. It is only an analogy, I am not suggesting for one minute that we should all take to booting our children about when they ask for a sandwich. But clearly the mare had reached the end of her natural tolerance.

When a child has left home and is then back again there is a sense of impermanence that floats about in the air. You know that they are back but it is not forever. It may well be that life is organised and that everybody has a clear sense of how long they will be back for and what is next on the to do list. Well done you. This has never really been the case in my house. This is not a grumble but merely an observation that each household is different and functions differently.

While your child is enjoying their time at home, but also wishing they were elsewhere, it can be a bit wearing living life as if waiting for the starter's pistol to fire. It is not an enviable time of life for a young person but it can also be a bit grating to hear continual sighs of 'I wish I was in…' 'When I was…' 'My friend…is just so cool' and knowing that a large chunk of your child is floating about somewhere that has no connection to you or the home. If it is any consolation, when they were away they probably continually talked of home and family and friends. It is just a way of letting people know of all the bits that constitutes their person and that they are not simply made up of the immediate environment and people surrounding them at that time.

There is also a mild notion in the air that, as a parent, you have absolutely no understanding of the world. It would seem that, all of a sudden, you have become devoid of all previous experience of life. It is just a way of our children letting us know that they have managed perfectly well without us and, as such, have a need to make continual statements of independence. We have all, at some point in our lives, thought that our parents have had their brains surgically removed. We never imagine, however, that we will one day be on the receiving end of such youthful wisdom. It is not easy but it is helpful to try and cast your mind back to your own behaviour. Anyway, this aspect of empty nest is around for a little while so this is just a taste of things to come in that department.

The sense of the current arrangements being a temporary state can permeate the air as it is quite clear that for a great deal of the time your child is wishing that they were somewhere else. It can be hard not to take this personally. It is not personal. It is just that coming back home after having left is generally seen as a backwards step in life. Even if a child has planned their time away and their return, it is not easy being at home once he or she has left.

It makes perfect sense that a child should leave the nest and return at intervals until they have mastered the art of flight. A bird does not leave the nest permanently on their first flight and all creatures take their time to reach independence, inching their way further and further from the lair until safety feels within their grasp.

Society is seemingly intolerant of children that return to the family home, although this may well change now that leaving home does not have to adhere to the strict time frames that it had to it in the past. It can be seen as a failure in some respects, which it is not. It is what it is and it is important to listen to your heart and head in equal measure, rather than the opinions of others. This is valid for both parents and children: their feelings about being back at home and not be influenced by what others or what society may think about that. This is your time and you will only have them for a little while.

Much as there may be a myriad of irritations piling into your world along with a spilling out of possessions, it is a time to be treasured. A time to use as a stepping-stone towards everybody getting used to the new way of being. When your child returns home again it will not be for long or even if it is quite a long time it will not be forever. There will be plenty of reminders when this period of time comes to an end. Plenty of boxes still to store and belongings hurriedly shoved away to remind you that they have been home.

Try and enjoy this time if you can. It is an important reconciling time where you remain a point of reference to return to and also to leave from. Home is still the launch pad from which they are practising their flight. Before you can blink they have found a solution to the next bit of their life and they are planning their next departure.

CHAPTER 5

THEN THEY'RE GONE AGAIN

Just as you have got used to the whirlwind of activity that a young person generally brings with them into the house then they are gone again! They somehow manage to leave a combination of chaos and tumbleweed.

There is the debris of them having 'packed everything away', which at best can be a very loose definition of packing things away. At the last minute they may declare that they are just going to have 'a little look' through bags and boxes and this statement still, after some years, makes a small panic rise up in my throat. My son's version of 'a little look' has always meant emptying the entire contents of various bags and boxes and spreading them far and wide about the house. However, I must add here that over the years this has improved immensely to his eternal credit (just in case he ever reads this!).

There is also a certain ambivalence on the part of the parent who is keen to tidy up after their child has gone but also not keen to 'tidy away' their children. While the mess is there it is, at least, evidence that they have been there even if they have gone again.

This is a complicated time as, just before they have gone, it is quite possible to have a mini re-run of the run up to departure. A grating of nerves and invading of each other's space so that it is easier to let go and say goodbye. Each of you may have come to realise that the act of separation is not only inevitable but may even be preferable for all concerned. It is also possible that you have connected with your child on a more adult level and that makes it harder to say goodbye.

One mum spoke beautifully of how her relationship with her eldest daughter had improved immensely upon her daughter's return from her first time away from home. Her daughter had been able to see her mum with all her qualities. All of the things that she had previously found so irritating, she could now see as her mum just caring for her welfare. All that nagging about coming home on time, doing her homework, being interested in who she was hanging out with, dishing out boyfriend advice. She could now understand the reasons behind it. They had spent a great few weeks together before her daughter had left home again on her next adventure. Although she missed her daughter she felt that they had been able to sort out differences in a way that would serve them well in the future and so she was left feeling a lot happier and with a lighter heart. She also spoke of her daughter being happy and said that it is so much easier to let go of your child when you know that they are happy and pursuing their dreams in life rather than struggling with their lot.

Her daughter, though, having returned home and had a great time while she was there, found it a real struggle to leave again. She said that she missed her mum and the rest of the family a lot more than the first time she left home when she was just keen to leave and get on in the world on her own. She felt able to love her siblings without feeling as though she was competing with them for her parents' attention and was surprised at how moved she was at the changes her siblings had made in her absence. When she left home again she also felt that she was able to keep contact with her siblings and have a relationship with them based much more on mutual respect and love rather than rivalry.

When a child comes home again and then they are gone again there is generally a sense of urgency about the whole procedure. They whirl themselves off into the ether, hurling forwards into their future and leaving behind a carnage of clues to signal that they have ever been back. This may not apply to all people. Some young people are very organised but even the most well organised child cannot avoid the fact that the years they are currently living, as they prepare to fly the nest completely, are imbued with transience.

Transience is the essence of these years. Transience and generally nowhere to store all the stuff that they do not need but do not want to throw away either. We all have a certain amount of belongings that are of no use but that we do not want to throw away. It is in a lot of people's natures to accumulate but now you have all the mess of a child, all of their stuff, with none of the joy of actually having a child there. The trail of belongings manages to hoist a new flag of sadness as you get used to their absence all over again. When your child has come back and then they are gone again it seems to add another layer to their absence. As ever, it is not straightforward.

There is a renewed sense of loss. Maybe not as acute as the first time, but there is loss all the same. One mum spoke of the house feeling empty when her child left for the second time and that it felt emptier than it had the first time as it was one step closer to them leaving the nest altogether. Although she did not feel as distraught as when her child had left home for the first time, there was a sense of the future looming ahead that did not involve her child. At least, not in the way that it had always been before. It is inevitable, and every time that they go it is one step closer to them having gone forever. Her child, however, who had found it hard to leave home the first time now found it much easier and was excited at the thought of getting on with her new-found independence.

It does seem that when a child leaves home again there is a general imbalance of responses between child and parent. Maybe this is the case all along that where one may feel desolate the other may feel delighted! Is this not the very nature of parenthood? We are led on an emotional rollercoaster from the day that they are born and continually adapting and reshaping the relationship in tune with events, progress and external forces.

At least when they are gone again you are prepared this time for the void that they leave behind them. Well, you think you are. You are ready to steel yourself for the departure and in some ways you already have a few tricks up your sleeve as to how to deal with the situation.

You may have found a few strategies that worked the last time, whether that was long walks, crosswords, wine, wild affairs or a combination of all of the above. Whatever works really is the answer. Turn back to tried and tested friends and family who are prepared to listen. Do not try anybody new at this point. I did this and it did not work. With some kind of misguided sense of trust, I turned to a person who was not only unable to manage the loss that I was feeling but they did not particularly care either. Choose wisely, this is not a time for people experiments.

I found a whole new sense of mourning when my son left home for the second time. We had always got on well but, by the time that he had got to the stage of leaving home, coming back and leaving again he had also actually become someone with whom I would most want to spend my time. I seriously enjoyed having him about. He had always been really good company but he was then becoming an adult whom I would want to actually hang out with. It is different.

Apart from grieving my increasingly diminishing role as mum I was also simply missing this really cool person. I missed him as a person and not just as the person that I had always known and loved but as the person with all the extra bits to him that he had found and embodied on his journey out into the world. It was fascinating to hear what sense he was making of the planet and to hear how his beginnings in life had influenced the decisions that he made, the people that he mixed with and the places that he went to. Personally, and I know that this does not apply to everybody, I felt a deeper sense of loss than the first time although it was slightly easier to manage as I already had a few tried and tested methods of empty nest survival.

When they are gone again it might be that you are able to add a few more ingredients to the recipe of 'getting through it' that you did not get round to last time. All of those things that you were thinking of doing before but felt slightly in limbo so never got round to. In fact, you can return to some of the lifestyle that you had started to carve out for yourself before your child came back again. It is not all bad and some of it is actually pretty good.

All of that space that seems to be empty can again be filled up with what you want to do. You can get back to whatever it was that you might have started when they left the first time. You can spend hours, days and weeks doing whatever it is that you want. You can go and visit people and not come home. You can get back to noisy sex. You can get back to eating what and when you want without checking in with anybody else if they want anything as well. You can start to look forward and see if there is anything that you might want to do in the future. It is the perfect time to throw the cards in the air and see what happens.

At this point in the empty nest process I actually sold the house and moved. My son has since told me that he struggled a bit with that one, and that he felt that he had a place to return to in the following years but not a home. My reasoning was that it was my time to do what I wanted and to make life a bit easier for myself financially and every other way. The place where we had lived had many ties, most of them good and some of them not so healthy. In order to be able to move forwards I felt that I had to cut those ties not just for me but also for my son. Short term pain for long term gain and all that. Hopefully in the fullness of time he will see that I was trying to offer him, as well as myself, freedom from those ties.

My son has spoken about how, having left home the first time, he realised that this was not enough to cement his new-found feeling of independence. When he left home for the second time he felt more determined than he had the first time. He also felt more confident in getting back out there and making big decisions about his life. Seeing me move house helped to reinforce his sense of independence and ability to get on with his plans. Although he was not particularly happy with the house move he also acknowledges that his unhappiness was, in part, also due to him getting used to doing things his own way and that it was not always easy.

Sometimes in the empty nest years we have to make decisions that fit in with what is going on with us as parents as well as what is going on with our children. While their lives are just beginning and there is a world of opportunities out there for them, ours, let's face it, are probably over half way and the clock is ticking. When my son had gone for the second time I started to feel a sense of urgency to get on with my life before it was 'too late'. Cue the mid-life crisis and it is no coincidence that empty nest and the, so-called, mid-life crisis often coincide. All of a sudden parents are faced with a life without their children, without their defining role as parent and there is a need to do something about it.

I sold the house, changed my job and got a puppy. My son declared that he had been replaced by a puppy and I declared that I had to look after something! We had always had a dog in our home and there was no reason for that to change anyway. These were changes that were happening in his absence and over which he had no control, which can be a frightening thing for young people when they are not yet anchored in their new life whatever that may be. It is a time for them that is hanging in limbo between the worlds of home and the nest and life beyond.

Exciting though it may be, it is not always comfortable. The same goes for parents but it is also an ideal time to cash in on the window of time that presents itself before grandchildren arriving and elderly relatives that might need looking after. It is a brief window and can disappear before our eyes if we are not careful. Not for nothing is this time of life called the 'sandwich generation' as you can be sandwiched between two generations that need looking after. Grab that window of opportunity and get out there, if and while you can!

One mum that I spoke to said that she and her husband were moving abroad to take a working opportunity that they would not be able to find in their homeland. They were of an age that if they did not take the opportunity it would be unlikely that it would come around another time. They have three sons, two of whom were at university and one was working. She spoke of the relationship that she has with her sons and the way she had nurtured and encouraged a sense of independence which they had embraced. They were all supportive of their parent's decision to move and were looking forward to visiting them in their new environment. The mum spoke of feeling happy with their decision but that she had come up against judgement and criticism from other mums who were at a similar stage of empty nest in their lives. This had caused her to doubt herself and also to feel defensive about the move that they were making, despite the fact that it suited them as a family.

I, on the other hand, came up against judgement and criticism for getting another dog, which was deemed to be a tie when I was meant to be making the most of my life. Actually, it is possible to make the most of your life and have a dog at the same time, I have found out! Parenting is, though, one of the arenas in life where it is possible to come up against criticism no matter what angle you take on your decisions. Someone will always have something to say about it. Listen to the people who really care and ignore the rest, I would say. There is a wise saying: 'Those who mind don't matter and those who matter don't mind'.

When a child leaves home for the second time any remaining members of the household, if there are any, already have the first time experience of how things might be. The situation is no longer strange to them and they are more easily able to settle back into the dynamic that was established before the empty nestee came and went again. Given how their temporary return may have unsettled the family, there may even be a sigh of relief. One young person spoke of her older sister coming back and leaving again. She said that she had just got used to being bumped up to head sibling status when she found that she was back down the pile again on her sister's return. When her sister left again she was happy that she was able to take up the role of older sibling to her younger brothers without interference. She also said that although things had settled back again afterwards there was also always a part of her that was waiting for her sister's return.

It is, indeed, that sense of impermanence that hangs in the air once a child has gone, come back and gone again. While the first departure may have had a precise return date, it is more likely that the second departure will have a looser return date arrangement. It is all part of the lengthy leaving home procedure. There is a feeling that, although things have seemingly returned to how they were the first time that they went, it is not forever and that it is part of our role to remain on standby. There can be a feeling of wanting to get on with life but that it is not quite the right time yet.

I say that as a mum who sold the house and moved, but it was still with my son in mind and I stayed within the area that was familiar to him. It might be that I did this as much for my own benefit as it was for his. It can be terrifying to see the world open up in front of you with all of its possibilities and options. Staying in the same place and doing the same thing can provide an anchor as much for us as it can for our children. A stalling for time before the inevitable moment when you are no longer the reference point to which your child returns.

As is only human nature, everybody is different. It is impossible to say that each person's reactions will be the same, albeit there may be a common thread running through the very nature of empty nest.

One mum, who has five children, spoke of feeling impatient and how she wanted to get on with her life. She said that she had given many years of her life to parenting and that she now wanted some time for her. By the time that she had successfully raised five children to near-adulthood she had had enough of having demands placed upon her and of never having the space either physically, emotionally or mentally to be able to carve out some time for her. She moved house and said that she would be responsible for the children still living at home but that the eldest three who had left home, come back and gone again, would have to sort themselves out. She had the feeling that she had simply exhausted herself of her capacity to keep looking out for her children in such a hands-on way. She wanted to get on and do the things that she had always wanted to do. She wanted to enjoy her career and her relationship with her partner and generally look to her own future. To an outsider this may seem harsh but it is only a parent who knows what they have given and what their limit is and, as I said before, parenting is also an area of life where others are quick to criticise and judge. It is very easy to bring up other people's children!

When my son left home for the second time I had a distinct feeling in my maternal belly that the cord was stretching to its inevitable breaking point. It felt as though it was leading to only one conclusion, which was that my time with him in the family home was gradually drawing to its natural end. I felt as though I had to carve out a life for myself in order to offer him the freedom of not having to worry about me. I was distinctly aware that he was starting to need me in a different way and it was my job to adapt to that without laying any guilt or pressure on him to do otherwise.

It is easy to understand parents who leave their child's bedroom exactly as it always was and maybe that is the right thing to happen for them and their children. For my son this was not the right thing to do. He needed to move on and I had the task of allowing him the space to be able to do that. It is up to each parent and each child to know and do what is right for them without feeling pressured by outside forces to do otherwise. The parents of the three sons knew that it was right for them to move away to another country. The mum of five children knew that it was right for them that she demand some time and space for herself.

I also spoke with another mum whose son is in his late twenties but is still not ready to manage entirely on his own. She has said that she will know when the time is right and stands fast in the face of western opinion that a child should have flown and gone by that age. There are many factors that might delay the process and, indeed, whether it is right for someone at all. Not everybody is so easily able to manage and overcome the hurdles involved with leaving home.

There is, as we know, a fair amount of maintenance and paperwork that goes into functioning as an independent adult. This takes a lot of getting used to and there are varying degrees of being able to manage forms and the suchlike among people. To some it will strike terror into the very bones, while others seem to manage with ease and navigate the stormy seas of bureaucracy without a tear or a whimper. I would say that this is unusual and that most people need to be guided through the delights of passport forms, having a phone connected, signing rent contracts, filling in university forms and whatever else a person needs to do when they are leaving home.

When a child leaves home for the first time there is a level of paperwork that is fairly inevitable. When they come back and then leave again the paperwork seems to get more complicated. Maybe this is in line with how much more adventurous and confident our children get when they are flapping their wings to fly. Just when we think that our services are redundant or at least are dwindling then this can be when the most demanding of dilemmas are placed at the end of the phone/Skype/text/pigeon.

Generally our children will manage to create situations with which we are not familiar. Or if we were familiar at one point in our lives then that knowledge will probably now be outdated and fairly redundant. Certainly most university information, if you have any, will be irrelevant to how the system now works. Dilemmas that we will now be asked to solve will be unfamiliar such as the visa system, buying a motor bike in Papua New Guinea, missing the last train across Siberia or losing one, some or all of the many cards that we now seem to carry about our person.

As with technology, I found that my son was far more adept at solving the situations that he found himself in than I was. I am often easily daunted by forms, and paperwork in general, so am able to provide an achievable benchmark to follow and exceed. Our children may be more adept than us at a few things that pertain to their generation. Technology probably being top of the list.

There is one area in which we excel, though, and that is that we know our children. We know what their limit is in terms of adventures, and what the very thing is that makes them unhappy and stressed. What may appear trivial to an outsider can be the very thing that we know will make our children weep. We are the people that they can turn to because we are the people that have known them the longest. We are the people with whom they can be small children and stomp and wail with no recriminations. We are the people they can phone and dump every last angst upon and the next day we will be as if nothing has ever happened. We have seen the full range of their emotions and behaviours and there is nothing that they can do that will stop us from loving them. They know that and this is the anchor to which they return. This is the reference point that they turn to when they are feeling lost or their wings are a bit tired from all that flapping.

So, we hear tales of how they are working hard and how they have no money to eat decent food. From this we have to resist the temptation to say 'Well come home then!' They are proving to us that they are managing on their own, that they are overcoming trials and they are also checking that we are still there should they need us. Much as you are trying to carve out a life for yourself, you have no idea what is going to be thrown at you from one week to the next. It is like being a parental goalkeeper, standing poised to catch your child before they hit the back of the net, waiting to pick up any pieces if and when that might happen.

When your child leaves home for the second time you know that they are stepping further away from home. They are carving out a piece of the world of which you are not a part. You are no longer the centre of their universe and neither are they of yours. From a parent's point of view this may take a lot more getting used to than for a child but this is essentially what is happening.

As a bird returns to the nest while practising their flight so does a child. When they leave home again they are almost bound to return. The cord is stretching further and further but it is still there. They are not quite gone completely yet but the distance is growing. And here commence the years of back and forth.

CHAPTER 6

THE PING PONG YEARS

The ping pong years are the years in which your child goes back and forth from the family home. You are never quite sure when they are going to arrive and you are never entirely sure when they are going to leave. I know that it took me quite a few years to stop ending up back on my parents' doorstep and I also know that I was always made to feel welcome. Since becoming a parent myself I have reflected on my parents' ability to manage my coming and going and also how they managed to deal with my not altogether conventional lifestyle choices over the years.

The ping pong years are also ones that can become more expensive rather than cheaper. Your child's increasing independence would indicate that they are also becoming more independent financially and in many ways they are. But become more expensive they do indeed.

Now the issues are with cars, flights, things to do with the home and maybe even the arrival of grandchildren. It is a time when you hark back with nostalgia to the times of just having to get another P.E. kit or pay for a school trip. In hindsight, that was easy but we did not know that at the time. There are times when you may have to, or choose to, contribute to an idea that your child has and is dead set on trying out.

One mum spoke of helping her daughter out with the finances to gain a teaching qualification that would help her find work when she was travelling. It was a struggle for her to be able to afford this but she wanted her daughter to maximise her choices and be able to take opportunities that may not have been available to her without this qualification. She did not particularly agree with her life choices but was keen to be able to help her out with the choices that she was making at that time.

It is during the ping pong years that your child may make choices that make you raise your eyebrows a bit. It is also the time when, however hard it may be, it is important not to show that you think that any of their plans might sound, or actually be, unfeasible. Even though a child's independence from the family and the four walls of home is increasing there is still a need for approval from parents.

Similarly a child also fears being rejected, the flip side of approval, by their parent if they present back at home with a whole new image and sense of self. It can be important to feel accepted and approved of by our parents no matter what age we are. I do wonder, though, whether the point at which we feel able to be our own person without the fear of lack of approval is possibly the point at which we grow up. Maybe this applies to the wider public rather than to our own parents, from whom we always seek an approving nod of the head. It might be that there never ceases to be something that settles within us when our parents are fully approving of what we are doing.

On a very superficial level, it could be the changing appearance of our child that may not tally with our own taste. We have all looked back at photos of ourselves and wondered why on earth nobody told us how ridiculous we looked. It is important, though, to be able to feel free to experiment with our sense of self during these years and experimenting with our appearance is a big part of that. There may be an element of being embarrassed by your child's appearance — in which case try and keep that to yourself. If they are wearing too much make up/have green hair/walk round wearing a onesie then this is not going to last forever and everybody needs to mark themselves out as different, or indeed the same, as everyone else at some point in their lives.

It is harder to watch and keep quiet when you can see that your child is potentially making a monumental muff-up of their life but that they believe that they are doing the right thing. Often it is when we see our own mistakes mirrored in the actions of our children that we find it the hardest to tolerate and stand by and watch. Every ounce of your being can be screaming out to stop them making the same errors of judgement that you did, and you see your own worst defects coming back to haunt you in the deeds of your own children. It can be easier to go through difficult times ourselves than to watch our children struggling. We are biologically designed to protect them from all hurt and tumbles but during the ping pong years our job is more to stand by and watch. Even if their choices may not be congruent with your own they are precisely that — their choices.

I have letters from my ping pong years that I had written to people and that I had never got round to posting. I look back and think: what on earth was I thinking about?! Or not thinking about, more to the point. There are some toe-curlingly, embarrassingly ridiculous ideas and plans in those letters. There were also letters from friends going through a similar time and their ideas were also totally detached from reality. We have all turned out alright.

The ping pong years are when a young person is finding their feet in the world and it is up to us to accept that along with every bump in the road. They are feeling alien enough as it is without us taking great pains to point it out.

I have letters from my parents answering questions that I must have asked in my letters to them. Their love and tenderness comes out through all those words and, years later, I can see that they must have been living my ping pong years with me to some extent. In their letters they also talked about home and what they were doing in their daily lives. Even now I can remember that as being a sanity lifeline at the time. I had a need to know what was happening back at home and to root a part of me in something that was familiar. It was an anchor from which I was able to explore and not come adrift.

My parents were the people holding on to the string of my balloon to stop me disappearing. My parents were not involved in my life to any great degree but they were an anchor in time. They also gave me a great deal of freedom to explore the world on my own terms. I feel privileged to have had this example and of being able to take from that to pass on to my own son.

Before becoming parents ourselves, our only experience of parenting is that of being on the receiving end of our own parents. We take what we know, what we feel has been useful and try to discard the less useful bits if we are mindful enough to be able to do so. If one generation has struggled to let go of their children then it is likely, although not inevitable, that the next generation will do the same. In the same way that family patterns are handed down, so is the difficulty of never being able to find our own place in the world if we are not allowed the space to grow and explore. In our family, independence has always been valued and encouraged but this may not always be the best thing for a child or for the family as a whole.

The different families with whom I have worked have taught me that there is no such thing as a standard formula. Each family brings its own histories and stories. Each generation adds another layer to that history and does their best to be able to bring out the qualities in their children. How we get to where we need to go is our own personal journey that we all have to take at some point or another, whether in bringing up children or working out how to leave the family nest ourselves. How we get to do this is influenced by how our own parents allow us to get there.

We are but a small cog in a great big wheel. Small cogs that fit in with everybody else just so that they are able to function. Each family unit functions with their own patterns. There are family patterns that we do not even know exist unless we take the time to sit back and really think about the way that our families tick over. There are behaviours that may have stood the test of time and generations regardless of how useful they might be and regardless of how they might tie us to behaviours that might be destructive or nurturing. The ping pong years are also about dismantling all of this, as parents and as children, and trying to filter out what we might take forward into our own lives.

The upside of dismantling our history is that we can take the richness that is there within every family somewhere and weave that into our future. The downside is that we can feel that we are left without a childhood once we have taken it apart to look inside it at length. That which we thought was our truth was in fact something entirely different.

One young person spoke very honestly about looking back at her own childhood with older eyes. Once she had reasoned on it and taken it apart she then felt as though she had then robbed herself of the childhood that she had believed that she had. All that she had relied upon to gain her sense of self, she then felt were false memories. Although she felt that it had been necessary for her, a bit of her wished that she had never gone digging into her past and that she could have back the innocence of childhood that she previously had. It may be that she was still trying to piece her memories together and that, in the fullness of time, she could make peace with conclusions that she had drawn.

It is, then, understandable if people leave it all well alone and cruise along on the ready-built ship of memories and patterns in the family. Not necessarily a long-term solution but understandable all the same. Why take apart what is so solidly in place? Why risk up-setting everyone and everything? Because we have a responsibility to our children to try not to pass down harmful patterns.

There are certain patterns that end up being sewn into our psyche, into the very fabric of our being. At some point, it is inevitable that we start to sound like our own parents and it is then important to work out whether that is something that makes you smile or strikes terror into your heart. Usually a combination of the two. It is not a particularly easy time but it is a sound investment in the future for ourselves and our children if we try and work out where our patterns come from and what purpose they may serve.

As I have come to learn, it is not easy to watch our children grow up and ping pong back and forth to the family hearth. Not every child does ping pong back and forth, but those that do seem as though they are being dragged in several different directions.

While home can be a safety net during these ping pong years it can also be somewhere that a child feels slightly imprisoned. Sometimes returning to the family home can be due to a lack of a decent alternative. Many children would rather be out there doing something else somewhere else but, for whatever reason, they have returned home. It can be difficult not to take this personally when, the whole time they are home, they are frantically researching a viable means of escape. This may become an increasing issue in our worlds as young people are finding it more difficult to leave home. This is the time to try and find a solution to all that angst.

One of the ways to maintain an element of harmony is to continually get to know your child. Relationships do not just happen, they take continual work and it is no different with our children. I do not believe that it is always enough to rely upon the fact that we are their parents in order to remain in touch with our children. There can be a danger of the person that we love the most becoming a stranger with whom we have nothing in common.

During the ping pong years with my son we made a conscious effort to continue to get to know one another. During these years there can be huge changes in the lives of children and parents and the changes can come about rapidly. There comes a time when it is important to carry on knowing that other person as they change rather than relying on the past to continue to forge the future.

With my son, we would have regular designated times to catch up. Not just on what was happening in our lives but also why it might be happening, what was influencing our decisions, what was new and what things that we had outgrown. It sounds serious but it was lots of fun and always food for thought. It would stop us from getting stuck in the past whilst also valuing the treasure that is shared memories.

The ping pong years become a time of tying in the past with the present and then eventually, into the future. By making a concerted effort to continue to get to know your child and also to let them know how you have changed then, hopefully, this might reduce the risk factor of your child returning to teenage-like behaviour every time that they come home. We all know of people, or even ourselves who return to some kind of childlike state, as that is the role that is expected of them. A parent can revert to being the parent of a child rather than being the parent of an adult as that is what they might prefer or that is what is most comfortable for them. We have all been there to some extent and seen it in ourselves or in our partners when they return to their family home and start behaving like children! I am not sure if we can escape this entirely but we can certainly tone it down to something that is healthy and manageable.

It is during the ping pong years that a blueprint can be formed for how the relationship can be in the future. During these years a friendship can start forming that differs from the parent-child relationship. A friendship is based on independence and is respectful of that independence and this is what marks it out from other relationships.

The ever growing independence of our children, much as it can be difficult to watch, is a thing to rejoice in and can also be a great deal of fun. They will continue to introduce you to people and situations that you would not otherwise have come across. They might have interests that would never have occurred to you and so you come across worlds that you might never have known about.

Parents that I have spoken with have talked about worlds that they have come to know through their children. The spectrum is huge such as acting, sailing, martial arts, dancing, meditation, medieval history, tree identification, shopping (lots of shopping), different types of music, festivals, medicine, hairdressing, modelling, swimming, the gym, trains, lizards, cats, technology and so the list could go on and on. For every parent there was something new in this world that their child had introduced them to — and that has to be a perk of the job does it not! You can end up visiting places that you may have never thought of seeing when you visit your child in their new or current home. I am sure that many parents of children at university got to know new cities that they would never have otherwise been familiar with.

One mum that I spoke to said that she considers herself very lucky that her children have never moved far away from home as they live just around the corner. She feels, though, that she has got to know her home city a lot better through them and has discovered places on her doorstep that she had never known were there because of being involved in her children's interests and friends.

It is during these years that your child will start to bring back partners to the home. They may have been doing this for a while but it is likely that during this time a partner will emerge that could be their life-long partner. And/or the partner that they have children with. The idea is to keep your mouth shut and the door open with regards to their relationships. There can be the screamingly obvious warning signs that a person in love may overlook. In the fullness of time they will thank you for pointing these out but on the whole it is better to keep your opinions to yourself and for your child to know that they can return home unjudged.

When your child has a partner the whole dynamics of the relationship shift slightly. One of the main things is that you hardly ever get to spend time with them on their own any more. One mum spoke about her daughter and how she actually misses her now that she has a serious boyfriend. She misses the time that they used to spend together that her daughter now spends with her boyfriend. She said that as her daughter has grown up they have become good friends and she now misses that even though she sees her daughter regularly. She said how strange it is that you can miss someone so terribly even though you see them almost every day.

There were many stories from different parents of their children bringing boyfriends and girlfriends back home and they covered the spectrum of humanity from hilarious, touching, sad to downright ridiculous.

One young person spoke of her sister's boyfriend being controlling and that her sister has changed since she has been with him. She said that unfortunately she seems to be completely in love and that the relationship looks like it will probably last for years. She feels that the only thing that she can do is stand by her sister for the times when she is hurt by what goes on in the relationship. She cannot talk to her sister about how much she dislikes her boyfriend, as she is frightened of her sister getting upset and this causing a rift between them.

And therein lies most parents' dilemma. Do we say something and risk alienating our children or do we keep quiet and hope that the relationship fizzles out, or just accept that sometimes children make choices that are not congruent with our own? I do not have the answers, I am merely posing the questions! The issue of children's partners, parents-in-law and combined family units is one of eternal discussion and also the material for many a stand-up comedy show. It is something that most households will face at some point in their lives. It generally kicks off during the ping pong years and so is good practice for things to come in the future.

The combining of two households is rarely going to be an event-free ride and there are so many factors to take into account. My main concern was that I did not want my son to ever be in a position of having to be piggy in the middle and feel that his loyalties were split down the middle between parent and partner. With a bit of compromise on all parts this does not have to be something that is inevitable.

One mum told a wonderful tale of her daughter who, many years ago, brought home her new boyfriend. The mother described him as dirty with long hair, and homeless. She and her husband looked at each other with wide eyes but welcomed him into the home. Over the years it has turned out that this young man who seemed, at first glance, to be the most unlikely candidate has become a loving husband and a wonderful father to their two grandchildren. The mum spoke of being so glad that she had not spoken out loud to her daughter of her first opinion and that she now could not wish for a better partner for her daughter. She also said that as he has no contact with his family she wonders whether this has made things slightly easier for them all and less complicated.

During the ping pong years it would seem that whatever your opinion is, unless it is sought out by your child, then it is better to keep it to yourself. In fact, there is a stretch of a few years when your opinion becomes pretty much redundant as it would appear that you have no life experience whatsoever. We have all thought, at some point during our younger years, that our parents were incapable of any valid thought process. That they were aliens whose conclusions on life were totally inconsequential. Now it is your turn. This is the time when your child looks at you and sees you as an old person.

One dad spoke of his children, who are currently going through the ping pong years, and said that he can see that they are now starting to treat him like an old person. When he is on the computer they look over his shoulder and offer comments on how he could do things better. When he is cooking they offer opinions on how he could do things differently and how whatever he is doing is 'all wrong'. He has tried to point out that he has managed to raise them to adulthood successfully without killing them off with his food but that seems to carry no weight with them. He said that there are moments, when he is in their company, that he actually feels that he is stupid as he is aware that this is how they regard him. He is a successful and clever man who is involved in local politics, with a sound knowledge of the world, both past and current, but this does not seem to hold any validity with his children.

It can be hard not to take offence and I am not entirely sure that this is one that we should let slip by. It is worth pointing out every now and again that you may appear stupid to them but that this is not necessarily the case. It is without doubt that our children will have gained knowledge and information in this world that we have not had access to and it is more than helpful for them to pass it on. What is not helpful is if they come across as if that is the only knowledge and information that there is in this world.

When they return home for the first time, and then during the ping pong years, they can become critical of how things are done at home. They have had their first taste of the world, especially if they have been travelling and been to places that you have not, and are then keen to impose their new found knowledge upon you and the family home. They have done things on their own, found out things about the world that you do not know about and all of a sudden it is as if you need educating about life, the universe and everything. With a little bit of encouragement this too will pass.

During the ping pong years it is quite possible that you and your child will be living the separation experience entirely differently. In fact, it is inevitable. The times when you are desperately missing your child will be when they are having a whale of a time in their lives and not missing home one bit.

The one time when you would like to have loads of contact with them is when they forget that you exist and you are superfluous to their existence. Alternatively, just when your child needs a refuge and a break from their rocky route to adulthood, may be when you are relishing your new-found freedom from parental responsibility. Just when they need to come back home and take stock of their lives, and be somewhere that feels infinitely less complicated, or at least links them back to a time in their lives when life felt less complicated, is when you are feeling ready to move forwards from all of that.

If you are missing your child then it is fine to let them know that, just as it is fine for a child to come home, or phone home, to say that they are missing all that is familiar to them. There is a difference, though, in letting a child know that they are missed rather than that you are miserable and lonely without them. Nobody needs that millstone hanging round their neck and guilt, whichever way round it is thrown about, is not a particularly pleasant ball to chuck at someone. Guilt, I believe, is the one emotion, above all of the other emotions, that causes the most anger and that is something we could all do without.

The ping pong years can last for ages, years. There comes a time, though, when your child is ready to make a home elsewhere rather than simply lodging elsewhere and the family home being their base. Everybody does it in their own time and there is no prize for being the first to reach the end of these years. Whenever a person is ready is the right time.

At some point home becomes a place that they return to as a gathering place and a point of reference rather than anything more permanent. Generally it is a gradual affair and you notice that each time that they come home they take a bit more 'stuff' with them.

There are some things that seem to need to remain anchored in the family home and the rest seems to get filtered out a bit at a time. The ping pong years are ones that are often noted by parents as feeling as though they are a storage zone. As you manage to whittle down the 'things' that you have managed to accumulate over the years, so you also begin to amalgamate what is theirs into your own. It can feel as though you are able to claim some ownership over the bits that have been left scattered around the house for years and you begin to forget what belonged to you originally and what you have acquired over the years of things being left for storage during the ping pong years.

For me it was books. I love my books and during my son's teenage years and the years that followed we swapped many books and it started to become a struggle to know what belonged to who. There were the obvious ones and then the grey area of nobody knowing who they belonged to originally. Each time my son came home and left again he would take a few more books with him and each time it felt as though I had been burgled! There were gaps on the bookshelf that seemed to symbolise everything that I was feeling at the time. It almost felt like a divorce as each time he went off with a few more things that belonged to him but that I had forgotten did not belong to me. Try, if you can, to take it in good humour unless, of course, they are running off with your credit card and car keys which is a different ball game altogether.

As things left the family home I tried not to let my son see how much I was struggling with it all but much as I tried not to impose any of my empty nest angst in his direction it was almost impossible for him to remain immune. He was gradually leaving home never to return. He would return, of course, but never in the way that had always been. There were times, much as I believed it was the right thing to happen, that I wished with all my heart that it was not happening.

The ping pong years are the lead up to the real deal, the final separation. All that happens during the ping pong years is a practice for getting out there each unto their own. The ping pong years can form the future and how we might come back together as adults with our own thoughts and ideas. Of course it is never too late to change the path that we take and also it is never too late to form friendships and relationships with our parents and children. It is helpful, though, to cash in on these years to use them as a blueprint for the years to come.

As the ping pong years draw to a close, as the last boxes leave the house and their base is established elsewhere we have to think about finally cutting the cord, setting them free and releasing them back into the wild.

The ping pong years are our opportunity to take stock of where we have arrived at as parents and how we can take the next few years forward without placing any unnecessary weights on our children's shoulders for them to carry. During the ping pong years we are the pole around which they do their maypole dance and weave their own patterns. As these years come to their end it is now time to let go.

CHAPTER 7

CUTTING THE CORD

Cutting the cord sounds a bit harsh and final. It is also a bit of a cliché to talk about cutting the cord, or the apron strings as they are more commonly known, but it is a necessary part of the parenting repertoire that is placed before us to navigate as best we can.

The origin of the idea of cutting the apron strings is thought to have come from a time when it was custom to use the strings of an apron as 'reins' for small children. To cut the apron strings was a sign of going from a dependent to a more independent child. Is that not the whole aim of parenting: to ensure that they are able to manage as independent beings? Along with many other points, indeed; but the ultimate aim is that our children should be able to grow up and, in their turn, function out there wherever they are and whatever they are doing.

The dictionary definition of being 'tied to someone's apron strings' is: 'to make or be dependent on or dominated by someone' and the origins of that are from 1535-45 so it is nothing new! We can console ourselves with that at least. It is a well-trodden path that we are jogging along.

Another definition of being tied to someone's apron strings describes 'a child who is so used to their mother's care that they cannot do anything on their own'. As with everything in this world, there is a spectrum that is vast upon which we all sit at some point either that suits us, or that we find ourselves at. The reasons are as varied as the people involved. The idea, though, that a child cannot do anything on their own (if they are otherwise able to do so) without the help of their parent should not be one that raises a cheer in the heart of a parent that truly wishes the best for their child.

There is also a great deal of difference between a person being unable to do anything without the help of their parent and that situation being brought about by a parent's behaviour. There are many situations when a child becomes an adult but remains dependent upon someone for their care for whatever reason that may be. Cutting the apron strings refers more to the dependence that is created by a parent.

It is generally thought of as a derogatory term for someone to be referred to as hanging on to their mother's apron strings. It implies someone who is an adult but is struggling to function as an independent adult. It also implies a relationship with their parent that is altogether unhealthy and that is not allowing the child or adult to grow and live their lives as we suppose they should. It conjures up an image of a person you would not want to rely upon to be able to leap to your aid in a crisis. Plenty of blame is laid at their door but they cannot be like this on their own. It takes a parent who is not willing to let go to create such a person.

Letting go is not easy. I think we could all testify to this in some shape or form. Whether it be a job, house, pet or simply the edge of the ice rink! At some time in our lives we have to let go of people or situations and letting go of our children is probably one of the harder letting goes to be had. Even during times when we have had enough of them and their demands, we still do not really want them to be gone. Or, at least, not gone in the sense that we are not needed anymore, for that is what the real letting go is all about. It can be tempting to continue to be needed as much as is possible in order to hang on to the title of parent in the form with which we are so familiar. The title in which we have invested so much time, energy and years and which now fits us like a second skin or maybe even better than our original skin.

From the minute that they are born they are preparing, and we are preparing them, for departure. The whole run up to departure, leaving home and ping ponging back and forth has all been in preparation for the biggest departure of them all. Leaving behind all that ever was and taking on the whole parent-child situation as it is now. On the face of it that seems quite simple, natural even, but do not be fooled. Many of us are hard-wired to be needed in some way and parenting is the perfect outlet for that. To be needed by our children feels like the most natural being needed that there is.

There is also the phenomenon of unconditional love — it is quite addictive. Parental love is instantly unconditional, unlike any other relationship in a person's life. The state of unconditional has to be nurtured within a loving and growing relationship with any other person than your child. That is not an easy thing to let go of. It does not mean, though, that you are letting go of that unconditional love — but you are letting go of the relationship in its original form that allowed you to provide love endlessly in a totally unquestioned and unquestionable way. The relationship as it has always been is at the end of its time and now moves into something completely different.

Wonderful, but different. To carry on providing in the same way that you did when your child was small and their every need was to be tended to, would indicate that the apron strings that tie your child to you are well and truly in place, knotted and double-knotted even.

There comes a point when, as parents, we have to step back and consider the bulk of our work to be done and hope with all of our hearts that our children are ready to tackle life's daily tasks on their own. All of that training in doing the washing up, the clothes washing, making cups of tea and all that nagging to clear up after themselves? Well this was what it was all about. Not just to install some measure of what is alright into them and not just to ensure that the house does not descend into being knee-deep in dirty cups. Not just because you were too tired/hung over/ill/exhausted to make the tea yourself. It was all to be able to move your child towards independence and for them to be able to accomplish daily living tasks in their own home, or even in the family home if they are still there. For them to feel that they are not still a child only able to survive under their parent's strictly nurturing surveillance.

Bit by bit as they grew up it was our job to relinquish the control on our children that was previously needed in order to keep them safe, to stop them running in front of a car or launching themselves out of windows. During the ping pong years, we are required to become more practised in the art of relinquishing control as our children set off into the world with their own ideas that might not be a match with ours. They might be with partners that would not be our choice. They might choose to dress in a way that we would not choose or mix with people that we would not have chosen for them. All gentle but vital practice in the art of backing off and getting on with our own lives and not trying to run our children's lives for them or to offer unasked-for advice.

It is not as gloriously simple as it sounds. It is not easy to stand by and keep quiet when it feels as though one word from us and their lives would run so much more smoothly. Much as we would still like to offer our wise words of wisdom, they are no longer needed in the way that they have always been. This does not mean that they will never be needed, but it is different. Cutting the ties allows that difference to emerge and for our children to be able to make choices of their own.

Cutting the ties can sound as though you will be casting your child adrift into the world without an anchor, on their own forevermore. It feels as though it is something that goes against the parental heart but actually nothing could be further from the truth. It is an act of kindness that lies entirely within a child's best interests, which is something that we strive for throughout their growing years so why should it stop now?

It can be easy to confuse cutting ties with our children with rejecting our children, which are two completely different things. It is one thing jetting off to the other side of the planet leaving no forwarding address and not wishing to be contacted ever again. It is quite another wishing your child to be a fully-functioning and useful adult in whom you have every confidence that they will make the right choices, if not now then at least eventually.

I have an image of my dad teaching me to ride a bike and of the very first time that the stabilisers came off. I remember being terrified that I would fall off, that I would not want to ride a bike again, that I would damage the bike and so the list went on. I was not a terribly confident child and this just felt like one step too far. My dad ran round behind the bike holding on to the saddle while I pedalled hard. I was half way down the road before I realised that he was no longer holding on to the saddle and I promptly fell off. I have an ever-lasting memory of him waving cheerily at me from the end of the road, fully confident that I would be able to manage on my own. It was his confidence rather than my own that encouraged me to get back on and try again, this time successfully.

This does not stop throughout life and does not stop at being able to learn to ride a bike. It is often other people's confidence in your abilities that spurs you on to be able to achieve things that you may not have been able to achieve otherwise. It is like the grown-up version of being cheered on at sports day no matter how well you consider yourself to be doing.

Cutting the cord allows a child to gain the confidence in themselves to get on with things on their own and to make their own decisions. It shows that, even if they do not feel that they are able to manage brilliantly, there is at least one person in the world who believes that they are able to. Is there ever a time in life when we feel that we are perfectly able to manage? Probably not, but it does help if you have people around you who are sending out all the signals that they have confidence in your ability to cope. In order to be able to demonstrate that confidence to our children we have to be able to let them go.

One parent spoke of the change in the relationship with her children over the years and of the hard lessons she has had in order to be able to let them go their own way. She said that she will never stop wanting the best for her children and feeling sick to the heart when they are in a difficult situation, but that she has learnt that she must allow her children to fail in order for them to be able to learn to stand on their own two feet. She said that it felt like one of the hardest things that she has ever done, but that it has reaped huge rewards in how she is now able to get on with her children who are all now adults. She has also seen the benefits for them and has seen their confidence in themselves increase once she was able to take a step back.

Likewise, one of her children spoke very wisely about the change that has come about in his relationship with his mother and what this means to him. He said that each time his mum solved a problem for him, without him asking, he felt as though she had stolen an opportunity from him. He also said that it made him feel less prepared for the world which he knew that he would eventually have to face on his own. He spoke very honestly about how each time a suggestion was made without him asking for it, or that a solution was found without his input, it was telling him that he was useless and unable to do things on his own. He said that he will still go to his mum for advice and he is now a grown adult about to start a family of his own. He is not, though, asking her to fix his problem for him but rather she is helping him to decide if an idea that he might have is valid or not.

The thoughtful young man now has a good relationship with his mum and greatly values her opinions but has said that it was a bit of a rocky route getting there and persuading his mum to let go. Luckily she was able to listen and not take offence with her son's observations of her behaviour. She was also big enough in herself to see that a change of her own behaviour would be a benefit for everybody. She was able to talk about the fact that what she was doing was meeting her needs rather than her children's needs but that, eventually, her insight and love for her children was greater than her need to be needed.

Many of us will say that we often turn to our parents for help and so it should be. It is important to have somebody to turn to at a time of need and who better than the person who loves you loads and is likely to give a positive response! Or at the very least they are likely to give you an honest response.

As parents, though, it is one thing to help out and quite another to allow your child to believe that they need you to the point of not being able to make any decisions without you. One is for their benefit and the other is for the parent's benefit. The temptation is to keep the roles as they have always been, which is that you are the one with the answers and the solutions. In that way it can mean that our role as parent never comes to an end.

In reality, we cannot hang on to that role if it means harming the very person that we adore. We need to get out the most enormous and most effective pair of scissors and cut the ties that are binding the child to our beings. Much as it might be the thing that we least want at that time it is the biggest gift that we can give to our children. It is gifting them the freedom from the ties that bind. 'If you love them let them go' is a well-known quote and now is the time to put that into action.

Cutting the cord does not mean cutting the connection. It just means cutting away any destructive patterns and any unhealthy interdependency. Our children's independence does not mean being disconnected. They continue to be connected to us, probably better than ever, and to need us, but in a different way.

As parents it is important that we ask ourselves whether what we are doing or saying is because it is what our children have asked for or because it is what we need. It is the time now to offer support, as this is what they need rather than parenting. Everybody needs support at some time in their lives and it may be that, as a parent, your support is ongoing throughout their lives to varying degrees.

I know of a mum who offers daily support to her children and is grandmother to several grandchildren. She offers an invaluable babysitting service and is a wonderful grandmother to the little ones, with whom she is in almost daily contact. On the face of it you could say that the apron strings are firmly in place but it is not the case. She does all of the things that she does because the children have asked for her help and she is in a position of being able to give her time to them. When she is doing something for herself she will say so and does not rearrange her life to the extent that everything she does is for the children.

One fundamental difference is that she acknowledges the children for who they are now and not for who they were as children. She listens to them and they listen to her when they ask for her advice. She does not see them as children who are in desperate need of her help, and her help only, but she sees them as the adults that they have become and that their quality of life is improved by her being able to offer her time and support. Her children are all capable adults who have, in their turn, become loving parents.

The relationships between them all have evolved to be able to encompass the changes that have come about over the years as is only natural. This has allowed them all to remain close but also for the children to have the freedom to grow up and be emotionally and financially independent.

The question of money and when to cut the financial ties is a whole other issue. There are many reasons as to why a child or young adult may need continuing financial support and this may become an increasingly common factor in the parent-child relationship as more young people struggle to maintain themselves financially. I guess that, as with many areas of parenting, it is important to ask why you are offering financial support. And also how is that financial support received: whether it is an agreed cordial arrangement, a temporary agreement at a difficult time, whether it is appreciated or merely expected.

There can always be an element of control involved with finances and the saying 's/he holds the purse strings' is often equated to 's/he wears the trousers' in terms of who is in charge of the household. Similarly, withdrawing financial support is known as cutting the purse strings.

The origins of this saying are thought to go back to a time before clothes had pockets as part of their design. A pocket was usually a cloth bag or leather pouch often tied to the belt at the waist and if it contained money it was known as a purse. One form of highway robbery was to be a 'cut-purse' and a skilled person could cut the purse strings without alerting the victim. The purse strings were simply the cords with which a purse was tied to the belt. It became, then, an obvious metaphor 'to cut the purse strings' meaning to deprive of finance. Clearly nobody is asking any parent to gallop up behind their child in a highwayman mask and whip their purses out of their bags unless it really takes your fancy.

It is helpful, though, to think about how offering continued financial support may be putting across the same message to a child as continually offering practical solutions in their lives. It can, as the young man said previously, lead them to feel that they are not capable of making it out there in the world on their own. There is definitely no easy solution here, no 'one size fits all' and each family has their own attitude towards money and what is an acceptable amount to be proffering at any one time.

As a child I loved getting pocket money but as an adult I never gave any to my son. Basically I didn't really have any left over to give and this may or may not have been understood by my son at the time. As he has become an adult I have enjoyed being able to help him out financially if I can and if he needs it but he has never come to expect it. He has always worked in part-time jobs from quite an early age and quickly came to appreciate that money rarely drops from the sky. I have always made a concerted effort not to equate any money giving with control on my part but I do know that there have been times when I have given him money as I have felt a bit guilty about something or other.

Guilt is a common emotion in parenthood and children know well how to play on this. Money very often comes into the equation and 'cutting the purse strings' is a strong message, saying that the dynamics that may have helped the family function at one time are no longer of any use. That the young people are above all of that and capable of making their own way in life.

As with cutting the ties or apron strings, there will always be times when a person needs to turn to someone else for support and financial support is no different. It may be that cutting the purse strings simply involves laying down a few rules and making a child aware that any money coming their way is a benefit rather than a given right.

One bone of contention within families can be when financial help is not equal between siblings. It may be that one child needs ongoing financial support, whereas another child is capable of managing their finances and so does not need any help. It may be that one child has always been more vulnerable, or perhaps unwell when they were young, and that the parent never gives up the role of being caretaker or rescuer for that child. It is hard when the ties are cut for one child but not for another and a child can see their parents going without themselves in order to support a sibling financially.

The bank of mum and dad can have an emotional cost as well as a financial one and it is helpful to consider the wider impact of supporting one child while considering another child capable of looking after themselves. I have seen how this has led to secrets being kept from family members in order to hide the amount of financial help that is being given and the growing resentment that can come out as a result of this. It can lead to separation between siblings, however hard a parent might try and avoid this happening.

Again, it is worth questioning whether bailing a child out every time that they are in financial trouble is really doing them any favours. And is it worth the cost to the other children? How easy is it to be completely fair? And, indeed, how feasible is it? A family is full of different personalities and circumstances that may not always require the same responses to each child. Perhaps communication is the key and most siblings would be happy if they just knew the real reasons for any disparities and were helped to understand their parents' motives for what may feel to them as something that is unfair.

As with everything, it is important to look not at what society or friends are telling you that you should be doing, but rather what your parental heart is telling you to do. Or maybe a mixture of all of the above, but especially listen to what your own heart is telling you. It is important to look at how you feel about any financial arrangements you may have with your child and whether they are of benefit to all of you rather than it being completely one-sided. Is it something that leaves bad feeling with anyone? Is it an arrangement that leaves you feeling resentful in any way?

With finances, I believe that it is helpful to apply the system used on aeroplanes with the oxygen masks. Parents are told to make sure that their own oxygen mask is secure and fastened before assisting their child. So with finances, the first advice may be to make sure that you take care of yourself and make sure that you are in a position to be able to help. It is of no use to anybody to go down the financial pan, with all of the consequences that this might entail, in order to ensure that your adult child does not get in a money muddle.

The idea is that our children become independent in all ways, including financially, and this dips up and down throughout their lives, as it does with everybody. There is rarely a time when things pan out indefinitely. If only that were the case. There is a time, though, when a child can be considered an adult and they can consider themselves to be adults. This also involves them being capable of taking care of themselves fairly consistently, blips aside.

As we see our children blossoming into the adults that they are becoming it is a time to be proud. As hard as it is to leave behind family life as it was, there are many more treasures to be had in the future and it is now a time when your child starts to become an inspiration to you. Perhaps they have always been that but now it happens in a different way. The relationship begins to become one that is more equal and one of equal compromise on both parts rather than it being so one-sided.

As a parent it is time to find additional meaning in life that does not involve being a parent. All of that practice during the years that they were leaving home, coming back and finding their feet in the world can now come to fruition. Of course we never stop being parents but it is different. The time of cutting the ties is one of recognising your child as a person completely in their own right. Your connection with them is a gift, an added bonus, rather than an inherent right. It is not a given and the relationship needs to evolve towards the future rather than focus on the past and what has always been. By cutting ties with our parents and children we are recognising their independence from us and celebrating the individuals that they are. They are always part of the family but they are also individuals within that family.

Families, as well we know, are complicated creatures. As we have said, each family has their own dynamics and the cord could be thought of as the invisible tie that binds us to those dynamics. Cutting the tie is also cutting the familiar ways of being with each other that may or may not be helpful.

We are all assigned a role in the family at birth that ties in with the people around us, and the roles that they have been given. These roles may not be our truth but they allow the family to function in the way that it needs to. We have all heard people describe family members as 'the clever one' or 'the black sheep' or 'the organised one'. If 'the organised one' then throws all the cards in the air and does something that is seemingly out of character, then that leaves the rest of the family wondering what on earth to do with themselves.

Alternatively, it gives the space for someone else to be 'the organised one', something they may always have wanted or known about themselves but not been 'allowed' to do.

We are never given a set of rules to live our lives by in the family. There is not a day when somebody sits you down and says 'right, this is how it works'. It all happens bit by bit from the minute you first open your eyes. Family provide your first view of the world and what you can expect from it. It is from family members that you learn what you need to do in order to get a bit of love and also what kind of person you are. This does not happen in an instruction manual but in a million different ways every day and it gets reinforced as the years go by.

As you grow older, the views that you were taught may not tally with what you have come to learn about yourself. Parents may not see you as the individual that you have evolved into but rather as the child that you always were. This is what cutting the ties helps to remedy.

Cutting the ties allows everybody to move forwards as the people that they are now rather than being stuck in the old familiar ways. There are shared memories of childhood that bind us together and these can be precious. Memories are important but they are not a place to get stuck in. There are many more memories to be made and had in the future that also shape who we are.

Cutting the ties does not mean that somebody has to be wrong and it is not necessary to get anybody, parent or child, to change their behaviour. It is about freedom from those ties to be able to evolve and come back together as adults.

CHAPTER 8

COMING BACK TOGETHER AS ADULTS

This is the good bit. This is where you really reap the rewards of all those years of hard work and worrying. Not to say that you ever actually stop worrying about your child but it definitely takes on a different form. This is the bit where you can sit back and enjoy the fruits of your labour and really step into a life of your own if you so wish.

Your child is no longer a child. They are their own fully fledged person and you now meet up as two adults. You will always be their parent, of this there is no doubt, but you are no longer responsible for their decisions nor, generally, have to pick up the pieces of any decisions that have gone wrong. You can support them and live any difficult times alongside them but it is no longer your responsibility to be rushing around after them with a dustpan and brush.

This is a time, I believe, that is also worth marking with some kind of ritual. Something that actually says 'Hurray! We made it and let's go forward as we mean to go on'. This was something that I was conscious of with my son but it is only in retrospect that I have seen how helpful it was to be able to mark this time and put a metaphorical flag in the ground at the end of childhood as we knew it.

We planned a trip away that would suit us both and that we could both do. We chose to go trekking as it was something that we could both do pretty much equally given our inevitable age difference. It would have been no good doing something where one would have ended up looking after the other and it was important that we went somewhere that was new to both of us. The point was to spend time together. I wanted to be able to spend some time with him to, again, hear what he was making of the world and of any hopes and dreams that he might have for the future. Any time that I spent with him in our normal lives was brief and often in the company of wider family and friends. It felt like there were snatched moments to be able to catch up but not really acknowledge that we were now at very different phases of our lives and that he was now an adult functioning in the adult world.

Many years ago we had worked out that there would be a month in the year 2012 that my son would be exactly half of my age. We had always promised ourselves that we would go on some kind of road trip to mark this event, which we did. It is in hindsight that I can see that the timing was perfect to be able to also mark what was happening in our lives in terms of him becoming an adult. We spent a month walking up mountains. It was ideal to be able to chat if we wanted and not chat if we didn't want to. We could spend time together or time alone and the decisions were made mutually. Tasks were assigned to each of us in preparing for our time away and that, too, was a perfect time to be able to recognise and acknowledge each other's strengths. My son was in charge of preparing the route (definitely not my strength) and I was generally in charge of booking things.

When we were away we were able to spend time talking about

his time growing up, what sense we made of it and also to be able to see things from our different points of view. He was able to hear what it was like for me as a mum during those years and apply adult logic to it. I am incredibly grateful to have been able to spend this time with him and it has served us well as we inch towards our even more adult years. He now feels more able to ask my advice without fear of being judged as a child but is confident that he is being seen as the adult that he has become. I feel that I am able to tell him things now that I would not have felt able to before

If anybody has a chance to be able to take time out to spend with their child as they are becoming adults then I cannot recommend it highly enough. It was not all sweetness and light. We argued, cried and laughed as we sorted through the years that have passed, but we were also determined that the years to come would not be tainted by dragging stuff that no longer serves a purpose into the future.

Often there can be incidents, or perceptions of incidents, that happen throughout the growing up years that unintentionally influence the way that we think about our parents or children. It is a gift to be able to sort this out relatively early on to stop it becoming toxic within the relationship. There may be a perfectly simple explanation. Sometimes it can be as simple as our children having the opportunity to see their parents as ordinary fallible human beings who, despite any failings, have their heart in the right place.

One young person spoke of reaching the age that her mother was when she was born. She found this difficult as her mum was someone that she had always very much looked up to and when she reached her age she saw her as a young person who was just trying to cope the best that she could with young children at that time. For the first time she saw her as someone who may not have all the answers or be able to manage anything that was thrown at her. She also said that it was a perfect time for her to feel able to ask her mum about things that had been weighing on her mind about her parents' divorce. She had a perception of her father that was not anchored in the reality of what had actually happened at that time. She was able to spend time with her mum clarifying what had really happened and how it had been for her parents.

This was something that she feels incredibly grateful for as she had begun to create all sorts of problems for herself that were affecting her life. She had blamed her mum for leaving her father when, in reality, it had been the other way round, and she was then able, with an adult perspective, to see the situation from both of her parents' points of view. She was able to see that she was leading her adult life influenced by her child's mind of what had happened and that she had tried to apportion blame where there was none to be had on either part. Her parents were human beings who had tried their best to make the relationship work but it was not possible.

Having since been in a long-term relationship herself she was also able to see that things are not always as black and white as they may seem to a child. The relationship with both of her parents has improved tenfold since then and she feels a great deal happier within herself and also within her relationship with her own partner.

The relationship with our children, as with any relationship, requires sustaining and working on. It does not just happen on its own, it needs nurturing and time spent on it for it to be able to thrive. There will, without doubt, be bumps in the road as with anything else in life, as that is simply the nature of life itself. With our children, though, having come such a long way since the beginnings, is it not worth a little bit of extra work even when it does not seem strictly necessary? Now is the time to be able to relish the luxury of spending time with someone that you have known for many years. And it takes dedication to keep knowing that person as they keep changing.

Now there is the joy of being in a parent-child relationship which is free of the ties of obligation and any perceived duties. If you play it right you can all rid yourselves of that sense of duty that so often ties us to our family and simply enjoy the benefits that blood ties can bring. How often do we think, oh blimey I'd better get in touch with my mum/dad/son/daughter? The thing with coming back together as adults is that, in theory, you don't actually have to. The sense of obligation is an unnecessary burden that we place upon ourselves or we feel that is placed upon us.

When we come back together as adults this is the perfect time to be able to say these things that are weighing upon us before we take them with us into all of eternity. With my son we tried to air all of that niggling angst that settles beneath the skin so comfortably. It is not easy and not entirely comfortable but it is well worth the effort.

During our time spent together up a mountain I was able to explain some of my reactions, and decisions that I had taken while he was growing up, and he was able to see that I was just doing the best that I could at that time. Also that I was just making it up as I was going along most of the time but always trying to make sure that what I was doing would be of benefit to him. There is a saying, 'it's not what you do it's the way that you do it' and our children can be tremendously forgiving as long as they are given the opportunity to understand our motives behind what we do.

As we come together as adults, our children are also able to see how we might have been when we were younger and this becomes something that is of interest to them. They have exited the phase, hopefully, when they believe that you did not exist before they came along and start to become interested in how you were as a child. They start to become interested in their roots. They have grown the wings that have allowed them to fly and now they start to investigate the roots that hold them firm.

We have seen our children grow up and become adults and, to some extent, they have also seen us grow up. As parents, we do an awful lot of growing up alongside our children and the people that we were when our children were small are hardly recognisable as the people that we become later on in life. Our children are some of the few people in our lives who have seen this transition and when we come back together as adults they start to understand the changes that we have made. With a few years behind them they can start to make sense of how the passing of the decades and the changes in society placed an influence upon us parents and what we were doing at the time.

When my son was young I was the only single parent in the whole primary school. It may have been the demographic of where we were living at the time that was unusual but it had an influence on how comfortable I felt within the school and also the way that my son was treated. I moved him to a different school in due course so that he would not feel that he had to work so hard just to prove himself to be worthy of anything, which was how the teacher made him feel. I moved him to a school with more of a mixed bag of families that was more representative of the world at that time.

We have talked about how the changing opinions in society have such an influence and, as an adult, he is able to see the impact that this had on him as a young child and the reasons behind my decision to move him to a different school.

It is not always just the dynamics within the family home that impact on our relationships. There are many different factors that can influence what path our relationship with our children might take. Not all of them are within our control but what is always within our control is how we deal with them.

When our children are young infants they are helpless and unable to take care of themselves. They have needs continuing throughout the years that also meet our needs as parents. It is almost flattering to us as parents to be seen as heroes through the eyes of our children, as we seem to have the solution to every dilemma and we have this great gift of being able to keep them alive. It is important to a child to be able to see their parents or caregivers as heroes.

When we come back together as adults it is almost as if they have seen through the tricks of the magician and, for a while, can eye us with an element of suspicion. They become cynical about their parents and it is almost as if they had been diddled in some way into thinking that their parents were super-human beings when in fact they were, and are, as fallible as the rest of the human race. There is a move from them loving their parents whole-heartedly to then simply tolerating them, generally during the adolescent years and in the run up to departure. This is not an easy transition for parents but there comes a point when they come out the other side of it all and the relationship becomes altogether more genuine.

When we come back together as adults our children have moved way beyond the phase of viewing us through rose tinted glasses and then with a wonky cynicism, to it being something that is reciprocal. Our children can now challenge us as any friend might and provoke us when we most need prodding. We can learn from them and what they have been seeing of the world. I do remember going to Rome with my son and being amazed by how much he knew about the history and the fascinating way that he was able to relay all of the information. I learnt more from him in one walk around the city than I ever did at school.

Our children, who may have always been fascinating, become even more so as we listen to what they are learning about, what they are passionate about and what really makes them tick. Although we may pride ourselves on the fact that we have raised a healthy human being, they have only ever really been on the receiving end of our parenting. Who they were in the first place is always who they were going to become. It is just that when we come back together as adults we can see them as having become more of who they were in the first place. There are, of course, events along the way that influence the course of our lives but who we are is essentially there at the first breath.

When my son was young he had all of the character and person-ality traits that he has now and they are now simply more so. He was always determined, buoyant and questioning but this has now come to the fore as he is able to lead his life as he wishes rather than having to squish himself into a family and school system that did not always listen to what he had to say. Parents will often exclaim that their children were stubborn/kind/level-headed/distracted from day one and that they can see this in them now and perhaps even emerging in grandchildren, as and when they appear on the scene.

Although children are obviously their own people from the very beginning, what they learn from us also adds to the melting pot of who they become and how they live their lives. Our children can learn as much from our faults as they can from our strengths and this is the time when they begin to realise this. They, hopefully, stop blaming us for not being the perfect human and start to see us with all of our flaws and accept that this is what goes to make up a person in their entirety. What a relief!

It is one of life's greatest lessons and gifts to be able to accept somebody warts and all and see that the person that you love has survived in the face of adversity, even when they do not seem able to manage. It is at this time when you are even able to ask your child for help with certain aspects of life. I am sure that more and more parents are turning to their children — certainly for technology advice.

Apart from the practical advice there is the advantage of having somebody to talk to who has known you for many years and is unlikely to judge you. I do not mean that we should be turning to our children for advice on inappropriate matters that we would only talk to our friends about, but they do have a measure of us that perhaps other people do not have. I have asked my son for his opinion when I have been dealing with work colleagues. He is able to add a perspective while also taking into account how I might deal with a situation. His is also a perspective that I have a great deal of respect for and he can be excruciatingly honest. Our children are able to give their opinion based on how they have seen us manage situations in the past. Also on how they have seen us manage as parents. They have themselves been on the receiving end of any of our directive behaviour or decision making, so are well placed to offer opinions.

Coming back together as adults is a time to be able to share the way that we deal with any outside or inside influences as a family. There is usually a uniting factor and one of those is often humour. Each family has their own sense of humour and it is often only with your parent or child that you can revel in that shared sense of humour. Things that might be off limits with most other people are good for a belly laugh with those with whom you have grown up.

Whatever has passed through the years of growing up remains as a sort of glue from which it is hard to detach entirely. There will probably never be anybody in the world that quite gets you in the way that your parent or child does. However strong your relationship with your partner or with friends, there is a tie between parent and child that stretches far beyond any other relationship in our lives. It may be that it is different with different children and with different parents but the tie is always there.

Coming back together as adults is the time when you are usually able to truly be yourself, however pretty or ugly that may be. Here are people that have seen you at your best, at your worst and everywhere in between. You have seen one another shouting, laughing, crying, throwing tantrums, head down the toilet being sick, healthy, elated, in the depths of despair and pretty much every other state along the human spectrum. You have seen each other make idiots of yourselves in a way that maybe nobody else has in this world. Being a parent and being a child involves a great deal of worry and self-doubt that perhaps only you and your child can understand. Nobody forgives you all your faults and revels in your successes in quite the same way as a parent or a child does. It is a relationship within which the most is expected and the most is forgiven.

This is a time to keep forgiving and, if possible, not take anything personally. As time marches on our children will have formed their own lives and possibly their own families. They will be experiencing a pull from many different directions and responding to the many demands that their different roles may ask of them. By now they may be a partner, an employee, a tenant and have various commitments in which we do not play a part. The amount that we may need to be in contact with them and the amount that they wish, or are able, to be in contact may not tally. This is to be respected and not made to be another source of guilt. It is possible to remain close to your children without them feeling smothered.

There are many ways of laying guilt upon children, or children laying guilt upon parents come to that. This is also a time when, as parents, we probably have fewer years ahead of us than we have behind us. Just as we are slowing down a little bit or thinking about things that we might have wanted to do in our youth that is now behind us, our children are reaching their peak. This is their time, let them have it. Do not assail them with your own regrets and rob them of the joy of youth by continually reminding them of how quickly it goes by and how easy it is to have regrets.

One parent spoke of how difficult she found it that her daughters were now in the peak of their physical beauty while hers was dwindling. She envied their youthfulness and said that while she could only wish the best for them and be happy for them, she could not help but feel a twinge of regret that she would never have that youth again. She also said that one of her daughters had pursued a creative style of life that she had never been able, or felt able, to follow. While she has always encouraged her daughter to follow her dreams and for her happiness to be her main priority she also felt envious that her daughter had managed to achieve what she had not.

While young people are so very much looking forward to growing up and looking to the future it is very difficult for them to be able to imagine that, as parents, we might be feeling envious of them. When we are older we can look back at lost opportunities and also at the way that we were raised ourselves. Usually every generation tries to give to their children what they felt that they missed out on themselves, whether that is love, material things or time spent with family. I have seen parents then feel slightly resentful that their children had the opportunities that they did not because, as parents, they have provided that.

It might be that a parent has always wanted to go to university but never had the money, opportunity or time to be able to do so. They may now be financing, for their child, the very opportunity that they would have wished for themselves. A young person cannot possibly understand that tumult of emotions that comes with a person giving what they have never had. Of course they will take it for granted; it is what they are living and it is of no help for any parent to resent them for this.

It is complicated, though, as is most of parenting. It is possible to love somebody to the ends of the earth, to wish the very best for them, be excited at all the choices that now lie at their feet but also to feel regret and a bit of envy. It does not mean that you wish it to be any different for your child, but maybe that you would wish things could have been different for yourself. It is how this is handled that makes all the difference, rather than denying that it is happening at all. Young people do not know yet what it is like to grow older and so risk feeling diminished and criticised by their parents.

It is a battle that is as old as time itself: the one of the youth hurrying to grow older and the older generation wishing that they were younger. The younger person sees the older person as settled, that they have choices, that they have control over their lives and get to do whatever they want to do. The older person sees the young person as being free from responsibility, having years ahead of them and being full of youthful bloom and vitality.

There is no answer except to accept that this is what is happening — it is part of life and not one to be ashamed of. A parent is not actually envious of their child, but perhaps feeling that they have missed out on something, have regrets and have lost something that they will never get back, such as their youth. Be honest. Just say what is happening for you. It will probably be helpful for them to know and also for them to be able to be more honest to their children when they are older.

Similarly, it is not helpful to keep giving your adult child continual comparisons with how you handled things when you were their age. Things have probably changed and it is undermining to have some-body keep talking about their own experiences when it is now the young person's time in life. 'When I was your age…' is actually really boring unless it is an anecdote that is actually sought out. For any advice to be listened to it needs to be asked for in the first place, otherwise it is just a noise like the radio being slightly off station, an irritation in the background that just grates on the nerves.

Coming back together as adults is generally a time when your child will ask for your advice and is interested in how you may have managed similar situations at a similar age — but it does need to be asked for. This goes for any people at any age I suppose and should not necessarily be confined to the parent-child relationship. We will all have met many a person who could do with waiting until they were asked before proffering their unsolicited advice!

Coming back together as adults, rather than a loss, is a gain. Often our children bring with them a partner who then brings their own family. Just when it feels as though the house is emptying itself of life can be when it starts to fill up again. You get introduced to whole new family systems free of charge. You are introduced to whole different family ways of life that are endlessly fascinating. Different birthdays and Christmas events, different holidays and different ways of doing similar things. All being well it is a combining that is harmonious and, if not, at least try and extract some humour from it!

Coming back together as adults can signify a glorious acceptance of all that is and all that has ever been. As young people we can expend an extortionate amount of energy in trying to get away from the very place that we eventually long to return to, which is home.

What we call home can mean a myriad of different things but it usually encompasses all the people that we hold dear and who have journeyed with us, for better or for worse. It does not necessarily mean home in the sense of a building, which can really just boil down to geography. It is the people that count and it is a celebration of feeling once again anchored back to the things that we know and that keep us safe, after several years of feeling as though the moorings have come loose. Once a young person has tried to make sense of what has gone before then they are not only more able to return but they often also want to return.

During the run up to departure and the ping pong years a young person will often focus on what is not there rather than what has always been there. It is easier that way to separate in order to be able to go out into the world and discover all the bits of themselves that can start to make a whole picture. There later comes a greater acceptance of parents and it becomes a wonderful freedom to realise that you can still love and admire someone even if you do not necessarily agree with them. As children it can be hard to appreciate the deep and unending pool of love that a parent has for their child. This can come later in life when, as parents ourselves, we realise what it means to actually experience that love for one person.

My son's well-being is the thing that is paramount in my world. I want him to be well. I want him to have a future where he feels happy and content within himself and there is nothing that I would not do for that to happen. However old our children get and however much we meet as adults, there is always a need for parents to know that their children are well.

When we come back together as adults there are so many things to celebrate. Apart from our freedom as parents to not have to run around after our children and to have the time to be able to pursue our own wishes. Apart from the shared humour and joy at being able to share your time with somebody that you have known for a long time. There is also the freedom for our children to be able to see us complete with all our foibles and still love us, and vice versa, although a parent's love will always be based on a far more primeval need and instinct.

After several years of wading through the empty nest experience with my son, coming back together as adults has been a wonderful and life-changing time for me. It really does feel as though we are moving on to the next phase of life and I feel truly blessed that we are able to do so. I am excited about the years that now lie ahead and am looking forward to being able to learn from my son and from what he has learnt out there on his adventures. I am very excited about becoming a grandparent one day but I have been told to hold my horses on that score!

Coming back together as adults feels like a gift and a massive reward. I hope that this waves a flag of hope for anyone out there going through the earlier stages of the empty nest experience. There is light at the end of this turbulent tunnel!

CHAPTER 9

FINAL THOUGHTS

Not everybody develops at the same pace and not everybody marches to the same drumbeat. We all know this but it can be easy to forget as we get caught up in who is doing what and when. We get wrapped up in the pressures of multitudes of exams and getting enough certificates to wallpaper the house with.

We tend to rush our way through childhood and schools are increasingly pressured to achieve targets in just about everything except breathing. Children, as well as teachers, are on the receiving end of that pressure. More and more we are pushing our children to achieve key milestones when perhaps children should be left to be able to reach these milestones at their own pace.

I am not advocating that we return to the days of simply labelling children as 'lazy' when they were not able to manage in the classroom. I can think of several people, at school at the same time as I was, who came out of the education system not even being able to read and were labelled as troublemakers.

I did not have an easy time at school but nobody really thought to ask why, as the pressure was on simply doing what you were told rather than seeking out the reasons for any behaviour. And nobody was particularly fussed if you went to lessons or did any of the work.

There was a brief waving of arms if you had broken some rules but nothing that particularly showed any interest in your welfare or progress. But maybe we have gone too far the other way. We have gone from, in the past, not recognising when children might be struggling, to now pathologising what may be a child simply reaching milestones at a different pace from the next child.

Over the years I have worked with many different children and families. I have seen children who could not string a sentence together way beyond the time when it was deemed 'normal' to be doing so but they have gone on to be perfectly sane and functioning adults.

In fact, I can think of one young girl who was taken round to all the professionals in the area as she was way behind in her speech and language. When she did finally speak it was in full sentences straight away and she now works within an organisation, giving presentations. It is no criticism to the professionals involved in her care, or to her parents who were simply pressured into believing that there was 'something wrong' with their daughter. In their heart of hearts they knew that she would just speak when she was ready. Knowing her now, as an adult, I can see that she would only speak when she had something worth saying, and she actually still enjoys simply listening to people, despite her work that involves her doing a lot of talking.

I worked for several years in the field of adoption and it was fairly standard for a child to be classed as developmentally delayed by the time they came to live with their adoptive family. Given the love and time to be able to fill in the gaps of their childhood they often quickly caught up with their peers. I am not dismissing out of hand any delays that children might experience but am just saying that sometimes we can be too quick to jump in and fix something that might just as easily right itself if the child is given the luxury of going at their own pace. Are children being herded along the milestone track at times before they are ready to move onto the next developmental phase?

In the same way that childhood can feel as though it is rushed through, sometimes it can feel the same at the other end when adolescence is asked to come to an abrupt halt. Behaviour is tolerated in a teenager during the years of puberty that is often expected to come to a stop when they reach 18-years-old. We all know that this is not realistic. Given the hormones that are raging around the brain of a 16- or 17-year-old, it would seem peculiar if those hormones automatically settled down by the age of 18. There is an expectation on young people to be more settled and mature when they hit the magic age of 18. It is hard to imagine how this might come about given the turbulence of the previous years.

Under most laws around the world, and especially in the western world, young people are recognised as adults at the age of 18. They are able to vote, leave home, join the army, adopt a child, get married, gamble, be convicted of a crime as an adult, work in a strip club, go bungee jumping, see a doctor on their own, rent a house, drive an ice cream truck and much more. Yet, young people still need a great deal of support beyond the age of 18 despite all their flapping of wings to escape the nest.

It can reduce a parent to sleepless nights and much tearing out of hair when they see their 18-year-old, and older, offspring behaving in a way that seems appropriate to one much younger. Parents can feel despair when they see that their child is still meandering about with no life direction well into their 20s. Many parents of 20-somethings devote a great deal of worry time to the fact that their children have not yet found a career that they would want to follow, that they have not yet split the atom, got married, bought a house or show any sign of wanting to settle down. There is good news! Research has shown that the brain, once thought to be fully developed after puberty, is still developing for several years after the age of 18.

The front part of the brain, called the prefrontal cortex, is one of the last brain regions to mature. It is the area of the brain that is responsible for planning, prioritising and controlling impulses and does not mature until at least the age of 25. Apparently, car rental companies soon cottoned on to this research and it is no coincidence that you cannot hire a car until the age of 25 and that the premiums for car insurance go down at this age. This part of the brain is the bit responsible for putting the brakes on risky behaviour, which includes reckless driving, and the skill of thinking things through.

Oh, how many of us parents have willed that bit of the brain to develop. Its lack of maturity can be responsible for precisely the sort of behaviour that we find so baffling in our children at a time when we had hoped that they had grown out of all that sort of thing. Phew! Sink back into the sofa and relax and wait for the time to come when the fog clears.

Luckily, the 20s are now accepted as being a time of self-discovery. It was not that long ago that a person was expected to be settled and producing children themselves in their 20s and, thankfully, the societal pressure is now off. It is now perfectly acceptable to be travelling or changing jobs, which is perfect. In fact, nature knows what it is doing. The fact that the brain remains unfinished in early adulthood means that it is perfectly designed to be malleable, to be able to adapt to different environments and work out what the world is up to. It is actually meant to be changing its mind all the time.

These are the years when a young person needs to work out what they are good at and what the world means to them. Typically these are the years when they asking themselves what they want to do and spend time trying to work out who they are. I do remember a parent talking to my mum when I was in my late teens. She was talking about her daughter who had gone to India to 'find herself' and she said this with much raising of eyebrows and with a conspiratorial chuckle added in by my mum. She obviously understood where this mum was coming from. What a brilliant idea I thought! Clearly I was at a similar stage of life and trying to work out what life was all about. And clearly both mums were at a stage of wishing that their offspring would just settle. Much as it may be frustrating to see your child meandering about and showing no signs of leading a responsible life, it is helpful if nobody panics about it, neither parent nor child.

This can be a stressful time for young people and, just when we think that our children are on their way to sorting their lives out, this is when they have car accidents and seem to be upping the alcohol consumption. Just when you had hoped that you could sleep easily at night it seems that the behaviour is more worrying than ever. Studies have shown high rates of anxiety and depression in young people, peaking between the ages of 18 to 25. This seems to level out by the age of 28 when the brain is formed and the prefrontal cortex has settled into some sort of shape. There is, though, further research to show that the brain is still evolving into its adult shape well into the 30s. It is still busy discarding information that is no longer of any use and building up useful information and strong connections.

It would make sense then that the brain becomes most efficient at that which is most practised. If a person practises rocket science then that is what they will become most proficient at. If a person practises sleeping their days away then that will create well-worn grooves in the corresponding bit of the brain. 'Use it or lose it' is the key message. The brain is often likened to a muscle that if not used will not strengthen and there does seem to be some truth in that. It would then correlate that if a muscle is used more in a certain area then that is where it will build up.

While the brain is still sorting out what shape it would like to settle in to, it is advisable to help it along with some brain stimulating activities. I can only guess that hours spent on social networking sites are not going to develop millions of helpful neuron pathways. It is not easy, as a parent, to coax children and young adults away from technology and towards some form of learning that might nurture dormant brain connections into blossom. You will not be thanked, in the short term, for pointing out that watching endless clips of strangers doing entertaining, but futile, things on the internet is not going to develop a brain that is going to save the world.

It feels like one nag piled on top of a great big pile of other nags. Maybe showing the brain research to young people may be of some interest? We can but try. Apparently we have a few years of not knowing what we are doing to practise our thinking skills in anyway, which comes as some comfort.

My dad always claimed that the real fun in his parenting life didn't start until we had all left home and then it was car crashes, divorces, poor life decisions and house disasters. If he was still here now I could show him the research so that he did not feel that he was in any way to blame. He always seemed very cheerful about it all though. I never felt that I was under any pressure to get my life sorted and embark on some sort of steady career. I am not sure whether that was because of his natural understanding and good nature or through lack of expectation. I got the distinct feeling, though, that he was reliving his younger years but through our eyes, the eyes of his children.

This, I am assuming, will come to all of us at some point. It is something that we do way beyond the time that the nest has emptied. We get to live the redundancies, nappy changing, house buying and other life events through our children and have to sit back while we watch them make decisions which do not always seem thoroughly thought through. But if the research is true to its findings then maybe decisions are not meant to be well thought through until later in life.

All of this wonderful research concludes that young people are far better equipped to be making major decisions when they are in their late 20s rather than in their early 20s, so that also leaves young people the time to go out and explore life. It also leaves parents to wallow in the reassuring joy that it is not their fault if their child seems to be living an itinerant life, or if they do not know what they are doing and seem to be continually changing their mind. It's normal! What a relief, and although it is helpful to read the research and be aware of brain developmental phases, it can be a lot harder to put this into practice.

This is where it is helpful to have gone through the cutting of ties so that we do not get caught up ourselves in the quandaries of our adult children. So that we do not continue to run around mopping up after them, or pathologise what is actually ordinary behaviour. I am not sure how we deal with any seemingly indecisive and unstable behaviour beyond the age at which the brain is deemed to have been fully developed. Maybe see them and love them for the adults that they are? Cut away any behaviour that is unhelpful? Maybe we can take a long hard look at ourselves. I know that at 50 years old I am still making decisions that could be easily queried. There must be some research out there somewhere to explain it away!

I believe that, increasingly, the concept of empty nest will have to be reconsidered. It has changed considerably in just a few generations, as so much has within the family environment. There is so much in the world that has changed in a short space of time and it makes sense that the family home and the dynamics within the family home are impacted upon as a result.

The life that we lead now is vastly different from the one that our parents lived, and attitudes have also changed. It was not long ago that mums had to give up their children rather than face the world as a single parent. Societal stigma made it impossible for them to lead a life with their children, that now, just a few years later, is seen as ordinary. We now look back in horror at what these women had to go through, and are still going through, as a result of the decisions that they were forced to make. Families are now made up of a glorious mixture of single parents, same-sex parents, step-parents and adoptive parents as well as birth parents and all of these are thankfully now seen as the natural mix that is family and mankind. There is a greater mix of dynamics to juggle but there is also a greater acceptance of the many ways that families are formed.

There is greater freedom in young people's lives today due to technology and communications systems. Hopefully, there is also increased tolerance towards different lifestyle choices, but there is also more pressure for young people in other areas of life. I am not so sure that it is harder now that it has ever been. It is different, but there are definitely certain areas of life that are now more difficult.

It is much harder for young people to set up home on their own now, probably harder than it has ever been in the western world. As the costs of living rise beyond that of the average wage so, more and more, young people remain within the family home. This is not always through choice and the family has to navigate their way through these circumstances to be able to make the living situation as harmonious as possible. Young people have to reconsider what their role is within the family home if they are going to be that much older when they are able to live independently. The concept of independence may have to change from how it is currently considered. It may be that parents have to reconsider the whole aspect of empty nest and how it is managed.

Young people are often no longer young people when they leave the family home. The increasingly popular gap year before starting university can be the only time that a young person is living in a situation where they have to look out for themselves. University can be an extension of the institution of school, perhaps giving young people a false sense of independence, albeit that those years are without doubt valuable growing up years. Young people do get to live a life away from home and the family and generally get to share a home with other people from different backgrounds. There is no doubt that this is a wonderful experience to add to the melting pot of life. It is, though, still a structured life that is under the tutelage of university tutors and deadlines for coursework. There are conditions and there is also a time limit, as the course will come to an end at some point.

It could be said that this is also true of the working life. That we are always under the tutelage of somebody somewhere. That there is always a time limit to what we are doing, along with an element of uncertainty. There is never any guarantee that a living arrangement will continue, whether an independent one or not. How, though, do rising living costs affect the ability of a young person to be able to leave home? It may be that young people will have to move in together more as we look towards the future.

When I left home it was the norm to have a room in a house and share with as many people as possible in order to be able to bring the household costs down to a manageable point. This seems to be fairly standard while people are at university but not later on when they are working. It has become more usual for young people to get places of their own, but these trends may reverse once more, as people are less and less able to afford the space for themselves. While certain aspects of society seem to be marching forwards, it would seem that there are other aspects that are taking us back to less comfortable times.

As university fees rise, and potentially make it less easy for the average person to access higher education, this might also impact on a young person's opportunities to experience life outside of the family home. University is certainly not the only way for a young person to leave home, but it is a popular version of carving out inde-pendence. My son did not go to university. School did not suit him and he did not want to carry on in the educational system without a specific goal in mind. He found an interesting way of leaving home, and travelling, that was cheaper and, in my mind, suited him far better. I do believe that we are in a moment of change that is going to impact on the opportunities for young people to be able to access education beyond school age and potentially impact on how young people are able to leave home.

As the noose around the benefits system's neck is tightened by government this will also have an impact on whether young people are able to live independently or whether they will have to stay in the family home whether they like it or not. Maybe this is way beyond the empty nest syndrome, but it certainly impacts on it and the phenomenon is increasing.

Adults will increasingly have to reconsider their lives, with regards to their own independence, in the light of having children still living at home. Parents may feel ready to move on with their lives long before their children are able to leave home. They may want to lead their lives without having to consider, subsidise and clear up after an adult child. In which case, what can be done to ensure the well-being of all concerned?

Children do not necessarily have to move out of the family home in order to learn how to be independent. They can do their own washing, pay rent, be involved in contributing to and sorting out the household bills and generally take responsibility for the mess that they generate. They can contribute to the maintenance of the family home and this will go far towards them learning about what it takes to keep a non-leaking roof over your head. Children could, potentially, become an asset to the family home. Asking a young person to take responsibility for themselves and not be a burden to the family home and purse is doing them a great favour even though they may not think it at the time.

There is a risk of children becoming infantilised by their parents as they remain longer in the family home. The temptation is for everybody to carry on as they have always done and for parents to remain in the parental role and not allow their children to grow up.

There are several successful sitcom programmes portraying the parental mix of resignation, worry, annoyance and perplexity at their children's inability to leave home and fend for themselves. There are stereotypes of young adults still in the family home who refuse to grow up. When I was growing up there was the sitcom Butterflies and now there is Gavin and Stacey who continue to pipe out this image through our television screens. Stories of adult children who refuse to leave the family nest but also continue to behave in a childlike way that is seemingly sustained by their parents' inability to let go. It is something that we find chilling and amusing in equal measure. It is something that mocks but also glamorises the eternal Peter Pan in all of us. What is it that we find so entertaining and yet, as parents, is also something that we dread?

Do young adults associate maturity with lack of fun? Maybe the more that adult responsibility is postponed, then the longer they can remain as children not deemed to be capable of shouldering responsibility. Are we, as parents, placing unrealistic expectations upon our children? Do children have unrealistic expectations of their parents? Whatever it is, it reflects a cultural change in society that children are spending longer with their parents now than they ever have done.

It has to be said that being a child now is infinitely more pleasant than it was in the past when you submitted to the older generation and went without privileges in order for the elders to enjoy their privileges. Children today perhaps have more of a sense that they have possibilities in their life rather than seeing their path as inevitable.

In previous generations there has generally been a sense of

expectation that a person's life will progress in an orderly fashion, such as finishing school, growing up, embarking on some sort of career, having a family and then retiring. This was the way of things and anybody who stepped off of that well trodden path was considered to be a bit of an odd bod. Every family has one or, if you are lucky, several. The one member of the family who did not conform to expectations and that everybody sighs about but secretly admires and envies. There was a sense that these people were not quite up to scratch, inferior in some way if they did not perform as expected, producing children and having a long lasting marriage. There is now a recognition that nobody trots along their life path in a way similar to the next person and greater tolerance towards a person choosing their own individual path is usually shown. We can but hope.

How will this, though, impact on society? Up until now people have been able to retire to be able to live on pensions that are supported by the next batch of young people who are treading the well-worn path that was recently expected of them. If everybody is in agreement that young people are still in limbo with their lives until at least their late 20s then where does that leave the current arrangements that we have? Will laws have to change accordingly?

There are laws that state that a young person reaches adulthood at the age of 18, albeit that their parents' income is still taken into account until they are 24 if they are applying for financial help. Young people in the care system are often out on their own at the age of 18, or even earlier, as they are then considered to be an adult.

Could it be that we are in a state of change now in the way that we consider a young person's route to adulthood? 100 years ago there was no such thing as adolescence and research into the developmental stages of childhood changed this. Maybe more recent research will again change the way that we view young adults if we are to incorporate this newly-recognised life phase.

This does not mean that children will no longer want to leave home. Do not panic! I believe that in the western world independence is something that is valued and children will always be encouraged to seek their way into the world. It may be that the road to adulthood is longer than we had previously thought. This does not necessarily have to be a negative.

If, as research is stating, young adults are unable to make tough decisions until their late 20s and their brain is only starting to settle into its shape by 25, then it may be that society will recognise this both in attitude and in law. If this is respected, as adolescence is now accepted and recognised, then young people will be given the space and time to grow up and reach adulthood at their own pace. This, it would logically follow, would lead to a land of adults who are more insightful, sensitive, thought-through and happier within themselves. This sounds like a mighty good thing to me. It could hail the end of the mid-life crisis as people reach their mid-lives having made decisions that they are happier with.

We are now living longer. Many changes in the healthcare system, diet and standards of living mean that we are able to enjoy more years than ever before. That does also mean that we have many more years to live with the decisions that we have made. I think that it is then helpful to be able to take a few more years at the beginning of life to consider those decisions, or even put them off for a while, before plunging into something that you may have to live with for the rest of your life. How many times do you hear somebody say that they wished they had been able to follow the work of a farmer/ architect/ steeplejack/ cook when they had been pressured to earn a steady living doing something that was way down their list of choices?

It is all food for thought. There are now more options open to us than ever before and my son has spoken of how daunting it is that there are so many options out there in the world. He has said that he has, at times, been almost envious of the generations where their future was predictable and inevitable and that you made the best of what you had to do. Mixed with the excitement of the future, as a young adult there is also a sense that the world is huge, as are the possibilities within it. I remember feeling a sense of panic that I was missing out on something out there in the world, and still do to some extent. I remember feeling a sense of urgency to get on with doing exciting things before life levelled out.

When does life actually pan out? I remember asking my dad this when I was a teenager. He said that it never pans out but that it is good to enjoy the plateaus, those moments when life is not firing anything to be dealt with. I have never forgotten his words. I had hoped that he would be able to offer a time in his life, an actual date, when things just magically sorted themselves but that is not the way of life. My son has also spoken of the ambivalence that he feels, in the midst of his enthusiasm, about the years that lie ahead of him.

Maybe that is good practice, as ambivalence is the very hallmark of parenting. It is very likely that your children, and family in general, are the biggest frustration in life, the very thing that makes you stay awake at night and gnash your teeth. The one thing that makes you rant like nothing else and turns you into someone that you are not particularly fond of. They are also your biggest achievement. There is no pride in the world like that of a parent. Nothing can make you smile and your heart warm like your children.

Along with the frustrations is a sense of wonder at all of the life potential that they have, the freshness that they bring to the world. They bring with them a sense of the forever after as the generations all roll into one another. And that, is the point of it all I suppose. That none of this ever stops and that the generations continue into the hereafter.

CHAPTER 10

TO BE CONTINUED

Parenting never stops. It changes but it never stops. It is a life-long contract whether you like it or not. As our lives change and evolve over the years, we continue to be parents to our children even if they are no longer children and no longer need our support.

What is the next step? We never really know what that is until we are able to look back on it in the same way that we are able to look back on our children growing up. Most of our learning is retrospective and the trick is not to let that reflecting on the past transform into regrets that stop us enjoying what is going on around us in the present time. As life carries on its merry path so we align ourselves with nature's twists and turns that take us to places that we had not planned and places that we had not even known existed. Children, more than anyone, are able to introduce us to worlds that we may never have known existed.

The next natural step in the parenting world after children have left home and become adults is for parents to become grandparents, but that may not necessarily happen. If it does, then we have a whole new avenue of parenting to navigate.

First of all, we do not have a choice about when we become grandparents. It is safe to say that this decision is entirely out of our hands.

It may not come at a time that is convenient. You may have just sold up and be embarking across the planet complete with long lost dreams and ambitions of seeing the world. You may still be working and not able to take time out to enjoy the arrival of your grandchild. You may be somewhere else entirely and not able to be involved. The potential circumstances are multiple although communication remains key.

With the advent of all kinds of communication methods it is pretty safe to assume that it is possible to keep in touch whatever the circumstances and geographical locations. My son was born in another country from my parents in the 80s and there was no such things as Skype (other methods of communication are available!), texting or video. It was phone calls and expensive ones at that. My parents and my son had the added complication of not speaking the same language, but they managed to circumnavigate all of that to remain involved and much loved grandparents. Where there is a will there is a way.

With families that I have worked with I have seen grandparents demonstrate the most stoic resolve around keeping in touch with their grandchildren whatever the circumstances. The fact that they are not just round the corner seems to make no difference and grandchildren seem to benefit hugely from having that link however far away they are. There is an adoring that comes from grandparents that is like no other in the world.

It is widely acclaimed that becoming grandparents is like having a second bash at being parents with none of the responsibility. It is rumoured that any lingering regrets over mistakes made during the parenting years can be remedied once the years of grandparenting begin. This is a chance to put right anything that you felt that you did wrong with your own children and a chance to carry on doing all of the things that you felt that you did right. Well that's a relief!

Grandparents who have spoken about the transition from parent to grandparent have regaled us with tales of the wonders of being grandparents, the lack of responsibility and all of the joy. They have spoken of there being a connection that is hard to put into words, one that spans the generations and taps into all of the nurturing and wisdom that age and experience can bring. With the hindsight that only passing years can bring they are able to see that the worries and pressures that they felt as parents were not necessary and many have spoken of feeling as though they have been given a second chance, not only to be with their grandchildren but also to be able to connect with their children again.

Who knows what can happen over the years? Who knows what decisions and life paths we might take and what the consequences might be? Sometimes decisions taken in life might lead to a rift between parents and children. Or if a distance has been allowed to appear then this can feel too wide to be bridged. Or opinions expressed cannot be unexpressed and this can cause hurt. Who knows? There are a multitude of different reasons why we might not feel as close to our children as the years pass. Becoming grandparents can be a chance to overcome any differences. It can be as if every-body is given a second chance to be able to move forward into the next phase of life.

Grandchildren put things into perspective, as does the birth of any new life. The introduction of a new person into our worlds can make us look long and hard at the way that we manage our lives and the relationships within them. Our gripes seen through the eyes of a newborn babe can pale into insignificance and this can heal any rifts that might exist, and people might find that they are willing to compromise more than they had first envisaged.

As with anything that involves children and families there are also complications. There are always complications. Rarely will you be the only grandparent. In fact, you could be one of several sets of grandparents if taking into consideration stepparents, extended families and also adoptive families with birth parents and grandparents. There could be a lot of competition out there that needs to be handled with kid gloves.

My son was born with Italian grandparents and I found myself launched into a whole new way of families that was not familiar to me. As a mum I was expected to hand over my precious newborn to the grandparents just when I wanted to lock myself away and simply stare at him all day. Well, that and sleep. I had no idea of the hierarchy of families and that I was merely a vehicle for producing a baby rather than anybody with any authority over the matter.

We managed to communicate all of our differences and find compromise. Not easy; nobody is claiming it to be easy. I certainly had many tears along the way. But I knew that I had to compromise to whatever degree and hanging on fiercely to what I believed in was not going to be helpful to anyone. What was the point of making everybody bend to what I knew and was used to if it only made everybody miserable, myself included?

And compromise is a bit of a key word in the grandparenting world and seems to be something common amongst all grandparenting experiences.

I have spoken with several people about their experiences of becoming grandparents, which go right across the board as only families can. One grandmother spoke of feeling that she was taken for granted and expected to babysit at a moment's notice. She felt that she had done her parenting and felt resentful that she was having to start out all over again. She had carved out a life for herself that she was very happy with and was not ready to give any of that up. She spoke of having dedicated years of her life to parenting her four children and that now was the time for her. Her view was that her daughter had made a decision to have a child. She considered this to be her daughter's choice and that, as a grandparent, she did not see why she should have to stick around to pick up the pieces.

Another grandparent felt that she was not being asked to help enough and was wary of seeming to be over-interfering. She felt awkward at having offered help and that the offer was not being taken up. She was aware that her daughter, as a new parent, had to find her own pace of life in her new family but felt that, as a grandparent, she did not know where she fitted in to all that. She desperately wanted to be involved but did not want to come across as bossy. As she became more assertive she found that her help was welcomed, but she could see how easily it would have been to have simply stayed in the background and for her wish to not seem interfering to have come across as indifference to the new parents.

One grandparent said that he felt that he was given a chance to be hands-on. He said that when he was a father it was not expected of him to change nappies and be present but that he had a chance to do all of that with his new granddaughter. He was delighted at finally being able to do all of those things that he was not expected to do, or didn't have the time to do, when he was a father. He also spoke of having the time to simply play with his granddaughter, which he could now see the importance of.

Another grandparent said that she felt nervous handling a newborn when it had been so long since she had been a parent herself. She spoke of feeling a lack of confidence in herself and her ability to be able to keep this little baby safe and come to no harm. She said that she had been a capable and dynamic mother herself but that when it came to being a grandmother she felt that it was worse than starting out from the beginning. She felt that she was being watched, and judged by the parents of the baby for her own perceived incompetency. Her lack of confidence was such that it was impacting on how much she saw her grandson. She wonders whether this might change as he grows older and more robust or whether something has been set in place that means that she has sidelined herself as a grandparent.

Another grandmother said that she felt that, as she was the mother of the father, she would be pushed out as a grandparent, that the mother's parents would be seen as a priority. She was fearful of being sidelined and did not know how she could overcome that without feeling as though she was barging in on the new parents' lives. She was also living some distance away while the maternal grandmother was living just around the corner. She felt as though the grandson was able to form a close relationship with his other grandmother while she remained a relative stranger. Much as she did not want it to happen she felt that she was in competition with the other grandmother.

One grandmother said that it was the best thing that had ever happened to her. She was in a position to be able to offer help but was also aware that her son and his wife were trying to establish themselves as parents first and foremost. She said that she felt a strong connection with her grandchildren and that it was a far more delightful and rewarding experience than parenting had ever been. She spoke of the time constraints when she was a parent and working, said that she was continually exhausted and felt that she only ever got to the end of each day by sheer good fortune. As a grandparent she has the time and energy to dedicate to her grandchildren with none of the pressures of work and time restraints. She spoke of the grandchildren having added a whole new purpose to her life.

She also felt that the birth of the grandchildren and the new role for her and her husband as grandparents had given a whole new lease of life to their marriage. They both have more energy and they have new things to talk about while also having exciting days planned out with the grandchildren. They both now see their son in a whole new light with renewed respect for the way that he has managed parenthood and being a husband. He asks for their advice, which is warmly received, while he also is able to tell them when he would like them to stay away.

A mixed bag for sure. It is fair to assume, though, that the 'to be continued' bit is preceded by an awful lot of hard work and good will. It does not just happen. The years that have gone before lay the foundations for a harmonious happy ever after. How the lead up to departure, the immediate aftermath, after a little bit of time has gone by, the ping pong years and cutting the ties are all handled will inevitably be carried forward into the 'to be continued'. Any unspoken resentments will continue to rear their head. Any unhealed rifts will present themselves in many a shape and form before they are allowed to be laid to rest.

There always feels as though there is so much room in life for regrets. It is important that we parents take time to congratulate ourselves on our achievements and not bow down to the guilt and self-flagellation that we are programmed towards. The 'to be continued' bit is our final chance to show our children how things are done. Show them that life does not grind to a halt at the first grey hair and that there is always a new way of finding out how to deal with stuff that life throws at us. If we have been on the receiving end of parenting that was not particularly brilliant, it is a chance to show our children that this does not have to define you. If you have experiences in life that are devastating and life-changing then it is a chance to show our children that it is possible to survive and survive well.

In the 'to be continued' bit we continue to be an example to our children even though this is much diluted from the years when they were dependent upon us for their every need. During the child-rearing years we were intent on giving them all of their needs but not all of their wants. Now is a time to show them that they can have their wants. Within reason of course. And providing their wants do not include wanting to take over the world or stride naked around Birmingham on a cold winter's morn.

We can lead by example and show them that they can want something and have it. Do not sit about with a big long list of 'I wish' and lament the joys of youth. It must be terrifying for young people to see the older generations full of misery and woe and saying that the best years of their lives are over. There are other things that we can do. Our bungee jumping days may not be at their peak but there is always a new dream out there to be had. Always something else to explore.

In fact, now is the time to be able to explore things that we would not have thought of in our youth. I would never have had the patience to sit for hours writing away when I was younger. Now I am glad of the excuse to sit in the warm and avoid all the frenetic action going on out there! The limits we place upon ourselves are often precisely that — limits — and they are not always justified. We are fed much stuff from society that makes us believe that our dreams are way out of our reach when this is not true. There may be material limitations, but are dreams always down to material gain and possibility?

I asked parents what they would wish most for their children throughout their lives. The first instinctive response in almost every-body was that they would wish for their children to be happy. That they themselves feel happy when they know that their children are content, no matter how old their children are. Without exception each parent spoke of wanting their child to be happy with the decisions that they had made in life and that they would have no regrets. They also wished for their children to be healthy. This is a lottery and usually out of anyone's control as to who draws the healthy straw or not. We wish for our children's health above our own. These are not things that can be bought with money.

When they went on to think further, then parents spoke of wishing that their children were able to buy a house, have lots of children, finish their education, travel the world and have flash cars. But that was not what came from the heart, it came from expectations placed upon us from outside forces. Our children may not be able to have the material things that we would wish for them and we believe that they would be happier if they had. And if it is the case, this situation may be only temporary. The point is that we still wish for their happiness and health above all else, even if material stuff is on the wish list.

I also asked young people what they would most wish for their parents throughout their lives. It may come as no surprise that their responses were remarkably similar to those of parents. They would wish for the health and happiness of their parents. Many wished that their parents would be able to enjoy their leisure time more after having seen them struggling with work for so many years. Many felt that their parents' well-being would afford them, as children, a certain amount of freedom, as all felt a level of responsibility towards their parents as they could see them ageing.

Or maybe it is that they become aware of time passing and the mortality of their parents. It is our parents who act as a buffer between us and mortality and as we all grow older there is a growing awareness of the possibility of that buffer being removed. Without exception all the young people delighted at the thought of their parents having adventures.

So we owe it to our children to give it our best shot! There is a poem that starts 'When I am an old woman I shall wear purple' and that pretty much sums up what we should be doing. The poem speaks of doing what we want, of not worrying about approval from anybody and generally enjoying life while it is there. We should give our children something to be embarrassed about and also to be proud of. They should be proud of their parents giving it their all and swimming against the tide of time. Give them something to rally against. Give them something to talk to their own children about, as the worst legacy of all has to be that of banality! Better for them to raise their eyebrows in resignation at your antics than to be coaxing you out of your front door to venture into the big mad world outside.

As we begin to realise that our lives are to be different from now on, so their lives are just beginning and it then dawns on them where they have come from. They become interested in their origins and it all starts to make a bit of sense. Even if it does not make sense now, at least they can gather together parts of the jigsaw for future assembly. They do not yet know that the jigsaw will be taken apart and put back together many times over before it makes any real sense, but there has to be a beginning. They will start to see where they fit in the grand scheme of things by piecing together their own generations of history. What this will mean to them when they become parents themselves.

What is the real meaning of parenting? The dictionary definition is: 'the process of taking care of children until they are old enough to take care of themselves', which is really the whole point. Interestingly, the first known use of the word parenting was not until 1958 so I'm not sure what it was all called before then. Maybe it was called 'just getting on with stuff'.

Parenting is, in a basic sense, about the continuing of the species. But it is so much more than that. It is a harsh lesson to learn, but which also makes perfect sense in an evolutionary way, that a person will always love their child more than they love their parent. As parents we accept this. We have all been given life, it stands to reason; but it is those who have given and nurtured life, and dedicated years to nurturing that life, who can have a window into the meaning of it all.

It is the 'ordinary' parent that is perhaps the greatest philosopher and who has all the answers to the meaning of life, the universe and everything. The very people who generally do not have the time to put pen to paper. And the very people who are so busy basking in the glorious simplicity of it all that it makes no sense to try and put any of it into words.

For all of you out there struggling to come to terms with the inevitability that is parenting, then I salute thee. Please spread your wise words and allow us all to share in your infinite wisdom that our children have tried so hard to grant us. And most of all, tell your children and grandchildren stories. Stories of the family. Stories of your adventures as a child. Stories of things that you got up to as a teenager (within reason!). Your favourite stories. Lots of stories to make them proud of who they are — stories to keep the magic in their world — and yours.

ACKNOWLEDGEMENTS

Firstly, thank you to Chris, my son, for his endless kindness and without whom, obviously, I would never have written this book.

Thank you to my mum and dad for giving me the freedom to explore the world in my own way and for not making me be any different.

Thank you to Jo for reading this through with her brilliantly analytical mind and painstakingly making corrections.

Thank you to Sam for all her encouragement and positive 'can do' approach to life.

Thank you to Amos (and Hannah!) for keeping me sane with gallops around the Essex countryside.

Thank you to my dear Tom dog for his patience and for sacrificing the odd walk when I was writing this.